BUSINESS ETHICS

BUSINESS ETHICS

Chris Moon and **Clive Bonny**
with
Sheila Bloom
Peter Desmond
Dawn-Marie Driscoll
Mark Goyder
Joel Hagan
Oonagh Mary Harpur
W. Michael Hoffman
Frances House
David Jackman
Keith Jones
Rushworth Kidder
George Moody-Stuart
Jane Nelson
Mollie Painter-Morland
Mike Peirce
Daniel Summerfield
Simon Webley

THE ECONOMIST IN ASSOCIATION WITH
PROFILE BOOKS LTD

Published by Profile Books Ltd
58A Hatton Garden, London ECIN 8LX

Typeset in EcoType by MacGuru
info@macguru.org.uk

Printed in Great Britain by
St Edmundsbury Press, Bury St Edmunds

A CIP catalogue record for this book is available
from the British Library

ISBN 1 86197 281 4

Contents

Acknowledgements

THE IDEA FOR this book came out of an ethics summit held at the Institute of Chartered Accountants in London in late 1999 and whose participants represented large and small public and private sector organisations with national and international operations. They met to share ideas and experiences in order to raise the quality of their own ethical thinking and, more importantly, to improve the implementation of ethical standards at work. Although there is a wealth of material on the theories and principles of business ethics, there is a dearth of practical help, and so this book evolved from a desire to provide frameworks by which organisations can set and instil ethical values and standards.

As managers of the project, there are a number of people whom we would like to thank for making it happen. First, the authors for finding the time in their busy schedules to write their chapters. Second, all the business men and women who gave us the benefit of their views on ethical issues and whose help in addressing how in practice businesses can operate ethically has been invaluable. Third, Marion Devine for her skilful editing of the book. And fourth, Stephen Brough of Profile Books for his tireless support and encouragement.

It seems beyond doubt that the issue of business ethics is being taken increasingly seriously by managers across the world as they realise that the reputation and the success of their organisations are linked to being able to demonstrate that their ethical standards come up to scratch. It is our hope that this book will help them to make sure that they do.

Chris Moon and Clive Bonny, June 2001

The authors

Sheila Bloom is Director of the Institute for Global Ethics UK Trust, a registered charity working in the areas of corporate ethics training and consultancy, values education and public policy. She is a fellow of the RSA and a founder member of its Forum for Ethics in the Workplace, and has a background in the arts, international advertising and marketing, and public affairs.

Clive Bonny is owner-manager of Strategic Management Partners, advising on business excellence & coaching managers in behavioural change. He is a trainer for the Institute for Global Ethics, a fellow of the RSA, and a founder of the Salopian Business Association, a non-profit community of small and medium-sized enterprises.

Peter Desmond is a founder director of Growth International, a firm specialising in performance measurement, financial management, group facilitation, ethics and organisational development. He has been involved for several years in the work done by the Centre for Tomorrow's Company on leadership, reporting and international corporate governance, and with drafting of the Commonwealth Corporate Governance Guidelines.

Dawn-Marie Driscoll is President of Driscoll Associates and an executive fellow and director of the Center for Business Ethics at Bentley College, Waltham, Massachusetts. She is a member of the board of governors of the Investment Company Institute and chairs its Directors Committee. She is a faculty member of the Ethics Officer Association and was the visiting John L. Aram Professor of Business Ethics at Gonzaga University.

Mark Goyder is Director of the Centre for Tomorrow's Company, which was established in 1996 following the Royal Society of Arts Inquiry, "Tomorrow's Company; the role of business in a changing world". He is the author of *Living Tomorrow's Company*, in which he sets out the philosophy behind Tomorrow's Company, and he is a regular contributor to such newspapers as the *Financial Times* and the *Times*.

Joel Hagan is Director of Strategy & Business Development for Andersen Business Consulting. He also co-founded Rigardi, a recruitment and HR consulting firm.

Oonagh Mary Harpur is Chief Executive of Enterprise Insight, a joint venture of the Confederation of British Industry, the Institute of Directors and British Chambers of Commerce to create a more enterprising culture in Britain. She is also Principal Tutor at Nottingham Law School's Centre for Law Firm Management, and a co-founder of Sherwood PSF Consulting. She is a committee member of the RSA Ethics in the Workplace Forum and in 1999 she led the National Forum on the purpose and values of business in Britain.

W. Michael Hoffman is founding Executive Director of the Center for Business Ethics at Bentley College, Waltham, Massachusetts, and has been a professor for 32 years in higher education. He was the first Executive Director of the Ethics Officer Association and is currently an adviser to its board of directors. He was a founder and President of the Society for Business Ethics and has written several books on business ethics.

Frances House is Director of Operational Policy for the Prince of Wales Business Leaders Forum. Her work focuses particularly on corporate engagement in the fields of human rights and enterprise development. Prior to joining PWBLF, she worked with the European Commission in Brussels and in Vietnam on the design and implementation of EC-funded humanitarian programmes with a focus on refugees.

David Jackman is head of industry training and business ethics at the Financial Services Authority (FSA). He was previously at IMRO, the Investment Management Regulatory Organisation, and was head of education at the Securities Institute.

Keith Jones is global head of social compliance for ITS, an international audit company Previously with SGS, he played a major role in the development of the ethical management standard SA 8000 and has many years experience of social responsibility auditing worldwide.

Rushworth Kidder is founder and President of the Institute for Global Ethics, Camden, Maine. Prior to founding the Institute in 1990, he was foreign correspondent and senior columnist for *The Christian Science Monitor* and, before that, he was professor of English at Wichita State University for ten years. Author of eight books and a regular contributor to newspapers and magazines, he serves on the Conference Board working group on global business ethics principles and the advisory board of the Kenan Institute for Ethics at Duke University. He is also a fellow of the George H. Gallup International Institute.

George Moody-Stuart is a former chairman of the UK branch of Transparency International. He worked for many years as an agro-industrial manager in the developing world, later becoming chairman of a UK-based company of consultants and managers. He was awarded the OBE in 2000.

Chris Moon is Manager, Business Ethics & Corporate Social Responsibility at Andersen. He represents Andersen on the Conference Board's panel concerning best practices in global corporate citizenship and he contributed to the Andersen/London Business School study *Ethical concerns and reputation risk management.* He taught the MBA business ethics modules at Imperial College in London for three years and has published in the *Journal of Business Ethics* and *Business Ethics: a European Review.* He is a fellow of the RSA and in 2001 he co-founded the European Business Ethics Network – Ethics Practitioner Forum.

Jane Nelson is Director, Business Leadership And Strategy of The Prince of Wales Business Leaders Forum. Prior to this she was the forum's director of policy and research, responsible for building relationships with international agencies and government bodies. She has worked with many organisations around the world, principally in commercial banking and in promoting public-private partnerships and corporate social responsibility.

Mollie Painter-Morland is Deputy Director, Centre for Occupational Ethics, University of Pretoria, South Africa. She is currently teaching business and professional ethics. She is a winner of the W. Michael Hoffman Prize for excellence in business ethics, and she received the graduate certificate in business ethics from Bentley College's Center for Business Ethics.

Mike Peirce is Chief Operating Officer of AccountAbility, a professional body committed to strengthening the social responsibility and ethical behaviour of the business community and not-for-profit organisations. He managed the development of the AA1000 Framework, AccountAbility's process standard in social and ethical accounting, auditing and reporting, and the launch of its professional qualification programme. He has also contributed to many initiatives concerning corporate sustainability and business-community relationships.

Daniel Summerfield is Corporate Governance Executive in the professional standards department of the Institute of Directors. He is responsible for developing and promoting the IOD's work in corporate governance through research, consultancy, publications, training programmes and presentations. He is also project manager for the independent director initiative, which aims to support and promote the role and contribution of non-executive directors, and is a member of several UK and international corporate governance working groups.

Simon Webley is Research Director of the Institute of Business Ethics. He has made a special study of business behaviour and published a number of studies for the Institute on codes of business ethics. He acted as rapporteur to the Interfaith group study of international business ethics and he compiled the Interfaith declaration on international business ethics. He is a visiting fellow of the City University Business School.

So does ethics affect the bottom line? Well, try arguing that it doesn't. You'll have to start by convincing yourself that trust, planning, or crisis management don't affect your ledger at all. Then you'll need to demonstrate that empowered personnel have nothing to do with success, and that neither customers nor shareholders are worth worrying about. Finally, you'll need to be clear that regulation carries no costs, that growth through partnerships is financially irrelevant, and that insurance is just a waste of money. Frankly, it's easier to make the case that ethics has a powerful, practical, and immediate impact on profitability.

Rushworth Kidder

Introduction

THIRTY YEARS AGO, Milton Friedman, a winner of the Nobel Prize for economics and a fierce advocate of free markets, argued that "there is one and only one social responsibility of business – to use its resources and engage in activities designed to increase its profits". In the years that followed many took the same view, but the ground has now shifted. Business ethics – the idea that businesses should not only behave according to certain moral standards but also demonstrate a level of social responsibility and accountability to a range of stakeholders that stretches from employees and customers to suppliers and the wider community – has risen up the management agenda. Why?

One powerful incentive behind this change has been the desire to avoid expensive court cases or the bad publicity and damage to their reputation that several well-known companies have experienced as a result of their perceived corporate irresponsibility. Shell, for example, suffered two blows to its reputation in 1995: one from its attempted disposal of the Brent Spar oil rig in the North Sea (even though there were many who believed that it was taking the most environmentally responsible course of action); the other over its failure to oppose the Nigerian government's execution of Ken Saro-Wiwa, a human-rights activist in a part of Nigeria where the company had extensive operations. And Nike faced heavy criticism when it was discovered that one of its suppliers was using child labour.

Increased shareholder scrutiny has put companies' ethics under a sharper spotlight. Annual general meetings can be noisy affairs these days, as activists take the company's directors to task for what they see as its unethical behaviour or lack of corporate social responsibility.

A more positive incentive behind the new focus on ethics is the growing evidence of the boost to brand value that can be gained if a brand is associated with ethical behaviour. There is also evidence that people are happier working for firms that they regard as ethical and, in the new economy, people are a firm's most valuable assets.

When the Dow Jones Sustainability Index was launched in 1999 *The Economist* argued that "Companies with an eye on their triple bottom line – economic, environmental, and social sustainability – outperform their less fastidious peers on the stock market." This may be why socially responsible investment (sri) criteria are now used by a number of leading fund managers. A Social Investment Forum survey found that 59% of occupational pension schemes now incorporate sri into their investment strategies. And new ethical indexes are on the way, among them ftse4Good.

The ethics movement has grown most strongly in the United States, perhaps because the risk of being penalised by the courts for unethical behaviour is greatest there. The Ethics Officers Association, which began in 1992 with just a handful of members, now has more than 700 members, and as many as one in five big firms has a full-time office devoted to the subject. But the business ethics movement is also gaining ground in western Europe and has begun to touch emerging economies, not least because of the desire of multinationals to make sure their supply chains come up to ethical scratch. Firms can no longer hide behind the "veil of ignorance" and claim that they had no idea what their suppliers were up to.

The concept of ethics comes from the Greek word "ethos", meaning both an individual's character and a community's culture. Generally people believe business ethics involves adhering to legal, regulatory, professional and company standards, keeping promises and commitments and abiding by general principles like fairness, truth, honesty and respect. The Institute for Global Ethics defines ethics as the obedience to the unenforceable.

It is certainly true that business ethics is a fuzzy area. No universal set of ethical principles exists and what is right and what is wrong often depends on the circumstances. The increasing realisation of this has led to a change in thinking about the most effective approaches to getting firms and their employees to behave ethically. Initial approaches were heavily based on "compliance", the creation of rules and systems that people and companies had to follow. But rules are hard to draft and can quickly become out of date, and systems can tie people up in bureaucracy and hamper business efficiency. Because of this there has evolved a belief that although some level of compliance will always be necessary, it is more important to instil ethical "values" into the corporate body and the employees that inhabit it. To do this successfully, businesses must have a vision about what they exist for, which is shared by everyone connected with the company. They must also have shared beliefs about acceptable (and unacceptable) standards of behaviour. These are difficult aims to achieve and require commitment, dialogue and moral imagination.

This book, which is written by those who specialise in or are closely involved in the field of business ethics, seeks, first, to highlight how important it is for companies to address ethical issues and, second, how firms can in practice go about addressing those issues. It is in four parts.

- Part 1 sets the scene. It looks at how the new economy has brought greater complexity to the business environment, changing the ethical dimension and raising new ethical issues. It goes on to outline attitudes and approaches to ethics on both sides of the Atlantic, and how organisations have gone about integrating an ethical framework into their business.
- Part 2 examines the interface between individuals and organisations. It explores the concept of ethical fitness and the role of leadership. It highlights the importance of effective corporate governance structures and gives practical guidance on how an organisation can define and clarify its purpose and values.
- Part 3 looks at the ethical problems, such as corruption, that companies may face and the issues, such as those connected with the supply chain, that they need to address when doing business internationally, especially in emerging economies or in countries with corrupt or repressive regimes.
- Part 4 gives practical guidance on how organisations can develop and implement codes of ethics, and it examines the various auditing approaches that have been adopted by companies seeking to account for their ethical standards and behaviour. Lastly, it looks at the role of an industry regulator in setting and enforcing ethical standards and, perhaps more importantly, in going beyond rules and regulation to get businesses to raise their ethical game.

Many people remain unconvinced by the business ethics movement. This book argues that business ethics matters because there is plenty of evidence that unethical behaviour can cost a company its reputation, hard cash and reduce the share price. Furthermore, companies that are perceived as ethical are more likely to build trust among their shareholders, employees, customers and the wider community, and this must be good for business. It also argues that business has a wider responsibility than just the bottom line and its shareholders. As an article on business ethics in *The Economist* put it, "Ultimately, companies may have to accept that virtue is sometimes its own reward."

1

SETTING THE SCENE

1 New economy, new ethics

Joel Hagan and Chris Moon

THE FUTURE IS NOT KNOWN, IT IS NOT WHAT OLDER PEOPLE THINK ABOUT
BUT WHAT YOUNGER PEOPLE DO.

Nicholas Negroponte

FOUR POWERFUL FORCES are driving change: technology, globalisation, the increasing value of intangible assets and the so-called "war for talent". These forces are reshaping the way companies manage their relationships in different local, national and international contexts with individuals and with other organisations. The success of these relationships hinges on the willingness of companies to become more open and accountable – explicit about the contract between them and their stakeholders; about a full range of objectives which include social and environmental impact, not just financial; and about the extent to which they deliver against their objectives.

Some people think that the new economy has been and gone; others think that it never happened at all. It doesn't much matter what you call the changing world. Nobody is arguing it hasn't changed at all.

Greater accountability requires business leaders to re-examine their attitudes and approaches, and to adapt and plan for new risks, challenges and opportunities. This chapter looks at the ethical issues involved and outlines the practical steps that managers can take to build more successful relationships with the stakeholders in their business.

Drivers of the new economy

Technology

Technology is revolutionising the nature and speed of communication within and between companies. The Internet, in particular, allows for huge amounts of data and information to be rapidly transmitted, anywhere, any time. This enables companies to forge ever-closer relationships with customers and suppliers, but it also poses risks, some of which are dubbed as "cyberliabilities". The Integralis Group, for example, surveyed 800 FTSE 1000 companies in March 1999 about their awareness of cyberliabilities such as "cyberlibel, copyright infringement, breach of confidence, negligent virus transmission, inadvertent contracts and computer hacking". Integralis found that although "the majority of directors accepted that e-mail is misused, they had no awareness of cyberliabilities ... and five of those six [listed] can be caused by any junior member of staff".

Recent pay-outs suggest that companies should be paying more attention. For example, petroleum giant Chevron suffered publicly when a few workers circulated two co-workers' e-mail titled "25 Reasons Why Beer is Better than Women." Some employees considered the message offensive and took Chevron to court, winning a $2.2m settlement.[1] In another recent case, a British insurance company paid out £450,000 for alleged defamation of a competitor by e-mail.[2]

Despite these incidents, many bosses are in the dark about the use of e-mail in their organisations. The American Management Association found that only one in seven companies reviewed messages. By comparison, Peapod, a London-based software company, found that 38% of major British corporations do so.[3]

Research into how employees use (or misuse) the Internet is revealing. Data from Content Technologies, a cyber-security software company, and a survey by NFO Worldwide for Elron Software found that:

- 50% of employees say they frequently surf the web for personal reasons at work;
- 85% of employees admit to sending or receiving personal e-mails at work.[4]

Surveys also show that:

- 66% of workers at big companies are aware that e-mail that is too embarrassing to pin on the office notice-board is sent via their employers' computer systems;[5]
- 50% of employees admit to receiving e-mails containing pornographic material and 62% of companies found employees accessing sex sites.[6]

How should companies respond to the misuse of communication technology? There are increasing numbers of reports of companies coming down hard on offenders; for example, Dow Chemical, the second biggest American chemical company, fired 50 workers and suspended 200 more for sending pornographic and violent e-mail. But the best strategy must be to stop such misuse occurring in the first place.

Monitoring e-mail use is an obvious step. Employers can buy specialist software. Put simply, these packages multiply the "find" facility in text processing to a vast degree. Some software screens e-mails using directories of undesirable words and phrases; other more complex software allows custom-built dictionaries of certain words, perhaps the names of competitors or project names, that alert the system and capture messages. These e-mails are referred to an administrator, who checks the message and either lets it through or blows the whistle.

E-mail filtering software protects equally against incoming obscenity, spam (unsolicited mail) and even mail-bombing, as suffered by two British companies that were brought to a standstill by 300,000 pre-programmed messages over a ten-hour period. Monitoring also prevents sensitive information from being leaked to competitors. Such software would probably have prevented employees of a multinational company from accidentally sending confidential personnel e-mails to a trade union; it could also have stopped a travel-agency worker from mistakenly e-mailing his firm's entire customer list to a competitor.

Some employees have taken offence and dubbed e-mail filtering products as "censorware", so the process in which a decision to monitor e-mail is implemented should allow such concerns to be aired and addressed. Simply informing employees about the nature and extent of e-mail monitoring helps to ensure its acceptance. In a survey of employees from 44 *Fortune* 100 companies, PC World Online found that 94% of respondents said they would agree to being monitored, as long as they were informed first. A mere 4% disagreed with the whole process of monitoring.[7]

A sound knowledge of the law is another important aspect of managing the ethical risks created by communication technology. But different rules in different countries can make things tricky for multinationals. American courts have historically taken the view that "an employee's right to privacy is trumped by an employer's business interests", and although staff have been challenging employer access to their e-mail since 1990, commentators say that no employee has yet won a case. Typically, two Californians fired for "inappropriate sexual humour" in e-mails who filed a counterclaim for invasion of privacy were told by the judge that they could not expect privacy in their use of equipment provided for company business.[8]

In Europe, however, a ruling from the European Court of Human Rights in 1997 determined that workers have a "reasonable expectation" of privacy in making and receiving calls at work.[9] With the implementation of the Human Rights Act in the UK, office staff everywhere will have to be told if their employers are monitoring their e-mails.

There are some practical steps that managers can take to tackle the ethical risks posed to their organisations by communications technology.

- Take conscious responsibility for the flow of information and data in and out of the organisation.
- Understand the legal responsibilities and liabilities of the organisation, taking into account national differences.
- Monitor the use of e-mail, using the most appropriate approach for the organisation's culture.
- Involve employees in discussions of the issues and the practicalities and encourage feedback.

Globalisation

Many forces are driving globalisation: communications technology, improvements in the transport infrastructure, deregulation, freer trade and freer movement of people.

The same conditions that have dissolved market barriers have also enabled pressure groups across the globe to link up and exert greater pressure on businesses. The environment, human rights, genetic modification and anti-capitalism have become much more visible issues thanks to the ability of groups to interact using the Internet. What once were local pockets of resistance, viewed as extremist, have become united and organised movements across the globe, and consequently more effective.

The ethical dimension of globalisation is beginning to be debated more widely. For instance, Colin Hines, author of *Localization – A Global Manifesto*, puts the case that there are downsides to globalisation such as damage to domestic industries and consequent local job losses. He also argues that the major shortcoming of globalisation is its tendency to increase the gap between rich and poor nations, a gap that has doubled in the past 40 years, regardless of absolute changes in prosperity.

D. Wheeler and M. Sillanpaa, in *The Stakeholder Corporation: a blueprint for maximising shareholder value*, calculate that the top 200 corporations in the world have sales equivalent to one-third of the world's total economic activity. As brands and products such as Coca-Cola and Microsoft establish themselves globally, local diversity is being affected, if not replaced, by global consistency. Making a successful global business involves working in a business environment which has many different languages, different cultures, different tax regimes and different rules and regulations, and which operates 24 hours a day.

Managers in global businesses can help their firms to be successful and to minimise ethical conflict in several ways.

- Know and comply with local laws, and regimes relating to finance, tax and employment.
- Be sympathetic to local custom such as dress codes.
- Be aware of global pressure groups that are relevant to their industry.
- Maintain and accommodate diversity within the company through working practices, management styles, employment benefits and performance management processes.

Intangible assets

The importance of intangible assets in the new economy has become ever more apparent. Traditionally, companies were valued in large part on tangible assets: according to bricks-and-mortar assets such as land, buildings, equipment and inventory. These assets all appeared in the balance sheet. In recent years value has been calculated based on a much wider range of assets but few of these make it on to balance sheets. They include:

- organisational assets, such as the ability to innovate, and various forms of intellectual property, such as codified knowledge about a product or process;
- customer assets, such as the number of customers and their loyalty to a business;
- employee and supplier assets, such as human capital (the level of knowledge and skill of the workforce) and relationships with key suppliers.

In 2000 it was not unusual for a company to be valued on the stockmarket at five times the value of its book assets. Despite recent market corrections, business success is driven by a company's ability to use its tangible and intangible assets in new, more inventive ways.

Intangible assets are, by their very nature, elusive – hard to quantify and track – and their value will vary according to the perception and attitudes of individuals and groups, including staff, customers, suppliers, journalists and analysts, shareholders and other stakeholders. Thus the part they play in ethical issues can be complicated. Even so, some practical steps that managers can take to reduce the potential for ethical conflict are as follows.

- Undertake reputation studies to understand how your brand is perceived.
- Actively manage stakeholder relations, monitoring expectations and performance levels.
- Account for the non-financial performance of the organisation and report on it.
- Develop and implement policies for corporate social responsibility or corporate citizenship.

The war for talent

Talented people, who possess knowledge, skills and ideas, are among the most valuable intangible assets of the new economy. And because they are increasingly in demand they are increasingly valuable.

A decline in the birth rate in developed countries has resulted in fewer people entering the workforce. Now that women make up around half of the workforce, shortages can in the short term be made up only by immigrants. The competition among firms for people with the aptitude, attitude and skills to help them succeed is fierce.

In 2000 18% of MBA students said they would gamble on a start-up; by 2001 the figure had fallen to 7%. But they have not lost their liking for the informal team-oriented atmosphere that many start-ups provide. Now they want it from the blue-chip employers to which they are returning.[10]

Retaining talented people is as big a challenge as getting them on board in the first place. It is now quite normal for people to change jobs frequently. McKinsey reports that the average executive today works in five companies but estimates that in another ten years it might be seven.[11] David Norburn, director of Imperial College Management School in London, comments:

> In the recent past, executives at board level averaged just 1.9 jobs on their CV. Today that average is up to three, still a small number, but all these new high-tech companies are changing the ethos.[12]

Many companies use financial incentives to help recruit and retain skilled people, such as pay rises that are ten times the rate of inflation or the potential for (even guarantee of) truly mouth-watering bonuses. Despite such inducements, there is evidence that many employees are dissatisfied with the deal they are getting from their company and lack commitment to their employer. A survey of 10,000 workers conducted in 32 countries by the Hudson Institute (based in Indianapolis) found that only 42% of employees believe that their employers deserve their allegiance.[13]

The 95 theses of the Cluetrain Manifesto[14] provide some insights into what employees want in these new economy days. Notably, they want their companies to learn to speak to them in a new way: honestly and humanely. If companies do not learn to do this then (thesis 89) employees will vote with their feet.

The Cluetrain Manifesto resonates with those who can be said to belong to "Generation X", after Douglas Coupland's book of that title. Generation Xers are often highly talented, independent individuals who share a set of attitudes, values and ideals. They are well informed and sceptical of institutions. They want immediate authority, independence and a voice in major decisions. They have technological savvy. And if they believe in what they are doing, they will throw everything they have into achieving their work goals.

Generation Xers believe that work is a two-way contract, a deal. Work is a means to an end for them, not an end in itself. The relationship they have with their employer must be a mutual, win-win one, in which their loyalty should not be taken for granted.

Increasingly, talented people will invest their energy and talent only in organisations with values and beliefs that match their own. In order to achieve this match, managers need to build cultures, compensation and benefits packages, and career paths that reflect and foster certain shared values and beliefs. This may require the following.

- Non-hierarchical organisational structures.
- A more explicit two-way contract between employer and employee.
- Awareness of and a positive policy towards environmental considerations.
- Using the brand internally, that is, with employees.
- A corporate culture that is underpinned by strong shared values and is supportive.
- A dynamic working environment.
- Incentive schemes in which employees get a share of the profits and/or have an equity stake in the business.

- Conditions that help achieve a healthy work-life balance.
- A system for regular measurement of employee satisfaction.

Studies show that companies that are most responsive to employees' needs have lower turnover in staff. For example, *Fortune* magazine publishes a list of the 100 best companies to work for in the United States, based on research conducted by Hewitt, a human-resources consultancy. Companies on this list attract twice as many applicants as their competitors, secure the most talented and have a staff turnover rate of around half that of competitors that are not on the list. Where skills shortages are most acute, companies are most responsive to their people's needs: 42% of the top 100 are IT or financial services firms.[15]

The 100 Best are rated highly by their employees because they pay attention to the issues listed above. For example, more than half of the companies offer share options to all employees. But perhaps more important in these high-pressure days is the way they try to help employees balance their home and work lives through things like flexible schedules and day care. In 1984 only one company on the list had on-site day care; today nearly one-third provide this. The 100 Best also try to satisfy their employees' appetite for intellectual improvement. More than half offer on-site university courses, and nine-tenths will contribute towards tuition fees – one-quarter will contribute more than $4,000 a year and one will contribute more than $15,000 a year.[16]

In the war for talent there are a number of things that managers should do to make sure they are well placed to hire and retain the best.

- Discover the reasons people leave the organisation and learn from them.
- Benchmark the total package (tangible and intangible elements) offered to employees against that offered by competitors.
- Find out what talented people want to encourage them to join or stay with a firm.
- Assess how the employment package being offered meets the package that people really want.
- Engage employees in the business, create a supportive and inclusive culture, and enable people to achieve a healthy balance between their work and the other parts of their life.

The rise of the economic network

Today's highly complex business environment is one in which organisations have to connect in order to survive, let alone succeed. Thus companies are linking together into economic networks and in the process transforming the way they do business.

In the West, the dominant business model was the autonomous business unit until companies began to work more closely with suppliers via electronic data interchange (EDI) and joint development programmes. In the East, the dominant business model is the network organisation. It has a long history and has involved the following.

- *Zaibatsu.* Japanese financial cliques of extremely tight family-based, industrial groups that dominated the economy before the second world war, acting in effect as venture capitalists.
- *Keiretsu.* Japanese industrial groups with their roots in the *zaibatsu*, consisting of member companies that rely on each other for synergy and are bound by the cross-holding of stock, which consists of a small percentage of shares (average cross-shareholding: *zaibatsu* 50–60%, *keiretsu* 10–20%).
- *Chaebol.* The South Korean version of *keiretsu*, in which companies are joined together in large interlocking corporations or conglomerates and are more closely associated with the government (because until recently most banks were government owned).

Now the global trend is towards companies that function as economic networks, made up of subsidiaries, partly owned operations, joint ventures and alliances, suppliers and customers. This link-up began through the formalisation of the supply chain, placing business units in groups along a chain of supply from raw materials to consumer products or services. Already this connectivity between an organisation and its suppliers and customers blurs traditional boundaries. A UK Department of Trade and Industry report explains:[17]

> To compete more effectively we have to collaborate more
> intelligently. Few companies have all the skills to make and
> market technologically complex products. Successful
> businesses depend upon strong teamwork – with suppliers,
> customers, joint-venture partners and universities and
> between managers and employees.

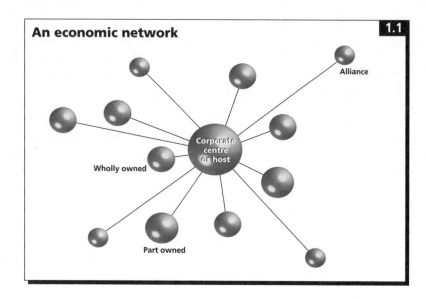

An economic network `1.1`

Alliance

Corporate centre or host

Wholly owned

Part owned

In April 2001, Booz, Allen & Hamilton, a consulting group, stated that the value of alliances in 2006 will be between $30–50 trillion. *PC Magazine* claims that over 20% of revenue earned by top American and European companies is generated from alliances, citing the main reasons as blurring of competitive boundaries, communication advances, and increased customer demand.

Embryonic economic networks consist initially of a corporate centre or host having stakes in related businesses (see Figure 1.1).

The next stage in the development of economic networks is for companies along the value chain to form close partnerships. Technology has been the catalyst for this development.

1 The transmission of data in quantities and at speeds has enabled outsourcing. Outsourcing in turn creates a web of organisations reliant on each other in a much more integral way than a traditional supply chain.

2 Application Services Providers (ASP). The ASP model takes this reliance even further by enabling the outsourcing of software that supports business processes and also business process improvement itself.

3 Digital markets. In these, the supply chain consists of many-to-many rather than one-to-one relationships.

Economic networks are particularly suited to the demands of the new economy because they can respond to complex conditions. The speed of technological and market change requires large organisations to be as agile as their smaller competitors. They have to play on a number of fronts simultaneously, mobilise rapidly to seize new opportunities, and gain quick access to diverse expertise and resources. Innovation and the sharing of ideas are helped by the fact that these economic networks function on the basis of relational interdependence rather than hierarchical control.

The significance of economic networks is that they are transforming the basis of relationships within and between companies. In the network model, suppliers, customers, alliance partners and employees exchange some kind of asset, whether tangible, such as specialised equipment or items of stock, or intangible, such as technical knowledge or marketing intelligence. These asset owners are becoming cross-owners. For example, employee share ownership schemes mean that employees are also owners (a problem partnerships have wrestled with for many years); suppliers and customers are also shareholders; suppliers are also customers. Managing all these relationships to keep everyone on board and avoid ethical conflicts has become increasingly important.

Value dynamics as a lens on the new economy

In the new economy the ability to forge successful relationships with a diverse set of stakeholders, including employees, customers, suppliers, pressure groups and opinion setters is crucial. How they perceive a business and what they say about it has a direct impact on its reputation, success and, ultimately, its share price. Yet how can businesses manage and protect these relationships, many of which are outside their direct control and may not even be apparent?

A framework called "Value Dynamics", developed by three senior partners at Andersen, helps to make sense of the relational interdependencies of the new economy.[18] Value Dynamics represents a business as an assortment of tangible and intangible assets.

On the left are the traditional assets that are listed in the balance sheet. On the right and in the centre are intangible assets, which generally do not appear in the balance sheet. Investments in intangible assets have traditionally been recorded as expenses in the income statement (profit and loss account).

Traditionally, companies have considered themselves accountable

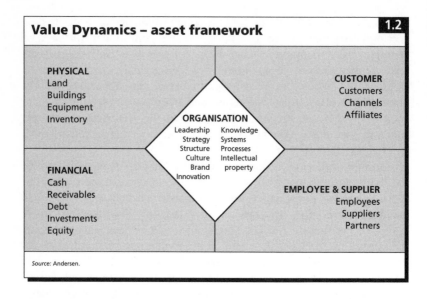

Value Dynamics – asset framework 1.2

PHYSICAL
Land
Buildings
Equipment
Inventory

ORGANISATION
Leadership   Knowledge
Strategy   Systems
Structure   Processes
Culture   Intellectual
Brand   property
Innovation

CUSTOMER
Customers
Channels
Affiliates

FINANCIAL
Cash
Receivables
Debt
Investments
Equity

EMPLOYEE & SUPPLIER
Employees
Suppliers
Partners

Source: Andersen.

principally, if not only, to their owners, the shareholders. Today, many take a broader view and think that businesses should be accountable to a wider range of stakeholders.

Value Dynamics provides a business case for stakeholder thinking because of the way it links stakeholders with tangible and intangible assets. Companies themselves consist of a group of assets (factories, technology, intellectual property, brand, and so on). Companies connect their group of assets with the assets of others and exploit the dynamics between these assets to create and realise value. For example:

- ◢ Starting on the firmest footing, shareholders invest their money into a company and expect a certain level of return from that money in the form of dividends and/or capital growth.
- ◢ Customers pay for goods, give their loyalty and enhance a company's reputation in return for goods or services that meet their needs.
- ◢ Employees provide their time, skills and energy in return for salary, bonus, career progression, learning, and so on.
- ◢ Physical assets, such as buildings or a fleet of vehicles, can be said to have two types of owners: legal and proxy. Proxy owners are those affected by the operation of the physical asset, such as a polluting factory. The rationale behind the idea of proxy owners

and strongly put forward by pressure groups such as Greenpeace is that we all own the environment.

As markets become more efficient, the relationships between an asset owner or stakeholder and the company become clearer and less secure. It has long been apparent that a provider of capital expects a return (though the globalisation of capital markets has made it even clearer). As industries deregulate and customer choice increases, customers have exercised similar rights and have moved their business when their needs and expectations have not been met. AT&T's customer satisfaction surveys famously told them there was no problem, but when the market opened up to competition defection rates were high. Perhaps most striking in recent years has been the employee/employer relationship: in the war for talent, job mobility is high.

The changes that have taken place imply that the owners of assets in effect lease their assets to the company for an expected level of return. Business managers therefore need to identify which combination of tangible and intangible assets are at play in their organisation. They should then take the following steps.

- Identify the owner of the asset.
- Contractually formalise and publish the relationship with each stakeholder.
- Identify any risk of not being able to fulfil contractual obligations.
- Ensure compliance with the contractual obligations.
- Engage and co-operate with stakeholders.
- Set targets.
- Measure performance, perhaps by developing a balanced scorecard of desired milestones and achievements based on the combination of assets in the business. (The idea of a balanced scorecard was introduced originally by Kaplan and Norton and was an important step in recognising that financial measures were too narrow indicators of business success. Kaplan and Norton added three dimensions: customer, internal, and learning and growth.)
- Report progress in achieving milestones internally to employees and externally to other stakeholders.
- Provide opportunities for feedback from all stakeholders.

The move towards greater accountability does not involve jettisoning sound economic principles, such as being in business to make a profit. Making money is being repositioned, not relegated. It can be likened to our perception of breathing: life is impossible without it but we do not live to breathe.

Acceptance of the legitimacy of stakeholder interests is gaining ground. The Centre for Tomorrow's Company reports that "40% of business leaders now believe that a company cannot succeed unless it has accountability that goes wider than shareholders".[19] The new languages of corporate social responsibility, ethical business behaviour, customer service, social justice, corporate governance, labour relations, community development and lifelong learning are all reflections of the same concept: responsibility towards stakeholders.

Signs of change are also encompassed in new actions. The consumer is more aware and more demanding than ever. Globalisation has brought increased prosperity to many, but it has become the focus of anti-business protesters, who see it as helping rich countries at the expense of the poor. Protesters took to the streets and rioted at many big gatherings of world leaders around the world in 1999 – Seattle for the meeting of the World Trade Organisation (WTO), London to coincide with the WTO – and 2000 – Montreal for the G20 summit, Prague for the IMF/World Bank annual meeting, Seoul for the Asia-Europe summit, Melbourne for the World Economic Forum, Nice for the European Union Summit.

Signs of change can also be seen in an explosion of work in developing and applying new non-financial measurement frameworks and associated processes: the acronym SEAAR (social and ethical accounting, auditing and reporting) has been coined for a segment of these measurement tools.

New economy, new ethical dimension

The new economy is changing the world of work and the people who work in it fundamentally. Technology, globalisation, intangibles and the war for talent are all driving the new economy and helping to create new corporate paradigms. In the new economy, business models can be seen as groupings of assets (or stakes) and businesses will need to be accountable to each asset owner (or stakeholder) in some kind of mutually agreed way. Wider accountability involves a wider ethical dimension that businesses must grapple with, and with this comes a greater risk of ethical conflicts that can damage an organisation. Avoiding them presents a new management challenge.

Reputation is a significant intangible asset and potential reputation damage is a key risk that companies need to manage. Reputation is nothing more and nothing less than the goodwill of all stakeholders. Therefore understanding stakeholders' views and meeting their needs is the way to shape reputation and manage the risks to it.

2 Attitudes and approaches

Chris Moon and Clive Bonny

BUSINESS VALUES AND PRINCIPLES REALLY HAVE NO MEANING UNLESS YOU
CAN PUT THEM INTO EFFECT. IMPLEMENTATION PROCESSES AND
APPROACHES ARE ABSOLUTELY CRITICAL.
　　Robin Aram, vice-president external relations and policy development,
Shell International

A⁣s EXPLAINED IN Chapter 1, the business environment is increasingly complex, and intra-corporate relationships are more important yet less easy to control. The day-to-day decisions and actions of ordinary employees can have far-reaching consequences. How can companies ensure that their business ethics are not abstract notions but practical guides to how employees act and behave? This chapter looks into the effectiveness of a range of approaches that can be taken. First, some people express their attitudes and approaches towards ethics issues in their workplaces. Second, the results of two independent studies are reported in order to assess the effectiveness of approaches being taken by companies to manage ethics in the workplace and what they can do to improve.

Get real

To be effective, ethical management must be concerned with how real people behave at work. At the individual level, an ethical issue and dilemma may surface suddenly, requiring an almost instinctive response. At the extreme, the decision made may be a matter of life or death. Police Superintendent John Slater, for example, had to decide who should live or die during a fire at a crowded boarding house. He recalls:

> I sent an officer upstairs to start evacuating tenants, and
> with another officer beside me we heard a voice behind a
> door asking "let me out, let me out". I put my gloved hand
> on the door handle, and the brass handle hissed as the heat
> met the glove. The paint on the door began to blister. I could
> have opened the door and got that person out. He was still
> alive. But had I done so, a fireball could have gone upstairs
> and killed the people above. I made the decision not to

open the door until I was satisfied everybody was out of the
premises. I listened to the person pleading and scratching
the door while about 40 people escaped down the stairs.
   The individual behind the door died. It was my decision.
A recurring nightmare I had afterwards was exactly the
same scenario, but the rest of the house was empty.

Fortunately, few people have to make such difficult decisions, but many will find themselves in situations at work where they must weigh different moral choices to determine the best course of action.

Ethics before profit

In 1991, The Body Shop, a well-known retailer, took the decision to phase out the use of PVC from its packaging and products. No item of PVC destined for sale has been purchased since 1992. This decision was taken as a precautionary approach to the environmental impact of PVC manufacture and associated health implications. Nicky Amos, head of business ethics at The Body Shop comments:

Whilst the company acknowledges the versatility of PVC as a
packaging and product material, our concern about the
social and environmental implications associated with PVC
overrides any decision to use it in our products, packaging
or shop fits.

John Lewis, a UK retail chain, had to resolve a number of ethical issues when it considered closing down a department store. One of its most founding principles is that employees are "partners" in the business. It also places great importance on other stakeholders, such as customers and suppliers, and its impact on the local community and the environment. Closing the store would have meant making 400 partners redundant. Instead, the company chose to place their interests above short-term financial considerations.

The chairman, Sir Stuart Hampson, explains:

The board deferred redundancies while developing a new
store in a strong trading location not very far away. This
meant over-manning by 100 people at a time when the
retail economy was suffering from a recession, but this was
a practical demonstration that we were a company which

recognised success depended on people, and we were
prepared to stand by our Partners.

Sir Stuart points to the role of the company's "constitution" in difficult ethical decisions.

Besides clearly defining Partner Rights, the constitution also
defines Partner Responsibilities to each other, to customers,
to suppliers, to competitors and to the environment. In this
way everyone inside and outside the business has a clear
understanding and expectation of each other and of how to
manage external stakeholders.

More companies appear to be embedding responsibility for ethics into business processes, so that decisions all around the company are made with ethics in mind. Mark Eade, head of ethics and reputation management at British Telecom, describes this approach.

Although our unit has the role of ethics champions – the
conscience of the company – we also get specific champions
within the operations. For example, we have a champion on
supply chain issues and a diversity champion. We use this
process to move ethics through the business and to get this
stuff into the bloodstream of the company. To make it work
you have to have a process by which ethical issues are
managed, measured and reported back on.

BP takes ethics seriously in its approach. There is a set of business policies covering five areas – ethics, environment, employees, relationships, finance and control. David Rice, director of the policy unit and chief of staff government and public affairs, indicates that ethics actually goes beyond the one area that they call ethics:

All of the policies together are about ethical behaviour,
which means doing the right thing. Do we have an ethics
officer or a compliance officer and so on? We have a
managing director and we have a number of champions
who are at group vice president level. Our policies we think
of and talk about as being beyond compliance so it is not
enough to be compliant, these policies are attached to every

*performance contract in the company and some of them
produce very stretched objectives and stretched targets.*

In this way ethically based management can shape an entire business: its structure, mode of operation, processes and culture. Mark Wilkinson, chairman of a privately owned wood furniture manufacturer, outlines some of the practical applications of his firm's ethical approach.

*For every customer order we plant a tree. We choose
sustainable raw materials only. We generate links with the
local schools, taking parties with primary school children.
We keep the local post office going by not using a franking
machine. If we used a franking machine the village post
office would lose our business and if it closed local people
would lose too. We do civic jobs in the community church.
We take older people in their 50s to be apprentices and it
gives them enormous satisfaction.*

In his case, commitment to the local community comes higher than commercial success.

*The club is the village, the club is life. If you're a member of
a club, it's wrong not to pay your subscription. In the game
that we are playing, money is what we use to keep the
score. That's all it is, it's just score keeping. We're not
playing in a vacuum, we're playing it with everybody else
in our community. They're all part of that game so the
benefits should come to all involved in the game.*

These attitudes highlight the way that ethics pervade daily working life. The moral choices taken by individuals directly affect their behaviour in the workplace. In today's complex environment, a rulebook or code of conduct is unlikely to be sufficient on its own to steer employees through various moral dilemmas. A number of different approaches can be followed to help them make choices and behave in a way that is consistent with the organisation's ethical standpoint.

Linking ethics with behaviour

Many organisations, particularly in the United States, have established ethics programmes as a way of minimising the risk of ethical misconduct or wrongdoing among employees. These programmes typically consist of policies, processes and educational and training initiatives that explain a company's business ethics. They clarify how these ethics should translate into operating procedures and workplace behaviour. The focus of ethics programmes is to gain "compliance", resulting in a heavy emphasis on rules and regulations.

More recently, companies have begun to favour a value-led approach. The emphasis is on achieving a match between the values of the company and those of the individual, so that the individual is intrinsically motivated to alter his or her behaviour. Robin Aram, vice-president, external relations and policy development, at Shell International, comments:

> We don't believe in requiring every one to comply with
> detailed rulebooks. We believe in a value-based approach
> that basically says you are being paid in order to make the
> right decisions based on a certain set of values and
> principles. I think value-based approaches are going to be
> more sustainable in the long term. That is the real driver – it
> will be more sustainable because people will intuitively,
> ultimately, instinctively do the right thing based on a set of
> values and principles, without having to go through the "oh
> is this right by the rule book".

Compliance programmes are usually expensive, but companies are willing to foot the bill because the consequences of unethical or illegal behaviour can be seriously damaging to their reputation and their stockmarket value. But many compliance programmes appear to be far from foolproof. Why?

Part of the reason is that companies have failed to gather systematic data about the effectiveness of their compliance programmes or about which management practices work best to create an ethical workplace. Many managers lack an understanding of what an ethics or compliance programme can actually accomplish and how its effectiveness is influenced by:

- the way it is designed;
- how employees perceive its objectives;
- different organisational factors.

To try and quantify these issues, two major studies have been carried out into the effectiveness of ethics and compliance programmes in the United States and the UK.

The US study[1]

Together with researchers from Pennsylvania State University and the University of Delaware, Andersen conducted a survey in 1999 on the effects of ethics and compliance programmes in six large American companies; 10,778 employees were selected at random and 2,883 responded. The study was designed to measure employees' perceptions, attitudes and behaviours. Perceptions are important because they influence attitudes, which in turn influence behaviour.

To encourage honesty, employees were asked about unethical behaviour that they had observed rather than their own behaviour. Employees at all levels of the organisations were surveyed in order to explore potential differences in perceptions between managers and line employees. The surveys were sent to employees' homes, rather than to work, to assure confidentiality.

The participating companies were in a variety of sectors. All had some form of existing ethics or compliance programme.

The survey explored the following three issues.

1 The effects of ethics and compliance programmes

Respondents were asked whether ethics and compliance programmes could alter the following attitudes and behaviours.

- Unethical or illegal behaviour
- Awareness of ethical issues
- Willingness to look for advice within the organisation
- Comfort in bringing problems and failures (bad news) to their supervisors
- Willingness to report violations within the organisation
- Commitment to the organisation
- Decision-making

2 The role of employee perceptions

In order to gauge the extent to which employee perceptions are accurate predictors of programme success, employees were asked whether they thought their company's programme aimed to do any of the following.

- Establish a shared set of company values to guide behaviour (values approach).
- Prevent, detect and punish violations of the law (compliance approach).
- Improve public image and relationships with external stakeholders (external approach).
- Protect top managers from blame for ethical failures or legal problems (protection approach).

(These four orientations are not mutually exclusive.)

3 The influence of organisational or programme factors
Respondents were asked about the organisational or programme factors that they thought most influenced the effectiveness of an ethics and compliance programme. They were asked to consider the following factors.

FORMAL PROGRAMME CHARACTERISTICS
- Employee familiarity with the contents of the code of conduct.
- Frequency with which employees refer to the code of conduct for guidance.
- Presence of a formal mechanism to raise issues or get help.
- Ethics and compliance issues included in employee performance appraisals.

PROGRAMME FOLLOW-THROUGH
- The organisation makes efforts to detect violators.
- The organisation follows up on reports of ethics or compliance concerns.
- There is consistency between ethics and compliance policies and actual organisational practices.

ETHICAL CULTURE
- Executive leadership attention to ethics.
- Supervisory leadership attention to ethics.
- Fair treatment of employees.
- Openness of discussion about ethics and values within the organisation.
- Ethics and values integrated into organisation decision-making.
- Ethical behaviour rewarded.
- Unethical behaviour punished.

- Unquestioning obedience to authority.
- Is organisational focus on: employees, customers and community, self-interest?

The survey findings

Many corporate ethics and compliance programmes rely heavily on a code of ethics and a telephone hotline or other formal reporting mechanisms to control employee behaviour. This study suggests, however, that these two mechanisms are the least effective influences on behaviour. Consistency between policies and actions, the rewarding of ethical behaviour and executive leadership's attention to ethics has the greatest impact on controlling employee unethical conduct. Furthermore, the mere existence of a formal mechanism by which ethical wrongdoing can be reported is not enough to encourage such reporting if the behaviour of management and the corporate culture do not support and encourage its use.

INGREDIENTS OF SUCCESS

The survey concluded that the most important factors contributing to the success of an ethics and compliance programme are when the general perception of employees is as follows.

- **Leadership:** that executives and supervisors care about ethics and values as much as they do about the bottom line.
- **Consistency between words and actions:** that management "practises what it preaches". This is more important than formal mechanisms such as hotlines for people to report wrongdoing.
- **Fairness:** that it operates fairly. To most employees, the most important ethical issue is how the organisation treats them and their co-workers.
- **Openness:** that people talk openly about ethics and values, and that ethics and values are integrated into business decision-making.
- **Just rewards:** that ethical behaviour is rewarded. This has greater influence on the effectiveness of an ethics programme than the perception that unethical behaviour is punished.
- **Values-driven:** that an ethics and compliance programme is values-driven. This had the most positive effect on all seven areas where an ethics and compliance programme can have an effect and resulted in:

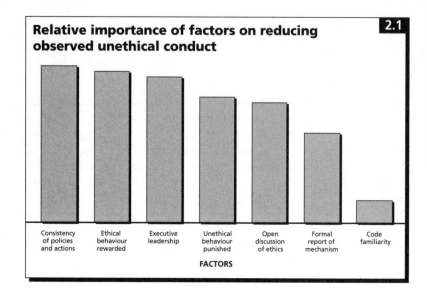

Relative importance of factors on reducing observed unethical conduct 2.1

Factors (left to right): Consistency of policies and actions; Ethical behaviour rewarded; Executive leadership; Unethical behaviour punished; Open discussion of ethics; Formal report of mechanism; Code familiarity

FACTORS

– lower observed unethical conduct;
– stronger employee commitment;
– a stronger belief that it is acceptable to deliver bad news to management.

Recipe for failure

The survey found that having an ethics and compliance programme that is perceived as existing only to protect the reputation of senior management may be more harmful than having no programme at all.

The UK study[2]

In 1999 a survey of FTSE 350 companies and non-quoted companies of equivalent size was carried out in the UK by Andersen in collaboration with London Business School and with the assistance of an advisory panel. The study examined how these companies were tackling ethical issues and how effective their actions were proving to be.

The use of ethics programmes

The use of business ethics programmes had increased significantly over the previous three years. Their components in order of popularity are as follows.

◪ Values/mission statements
◪ Codes of conduct
◪ Consideration of stakeholders' needs
◪ Periodic declarations/acknowledgements of compliance
◪ Reporting/advice channels (eg hotlines, compliance officer)
◪ Feedback mechanisms (eg surveys, focus groups)
◪ Employees/departments with ethics responsibility
◪ Business ethics training
◪ Inclusion of ethical criteria in performance reviews of divisions/functions
◪ Inclusion of ethical criteria in employee appraisal/reward systems
◪ Assessment of business ethics activities by external bodies

Four in five companies (78%) used codes of conduct, compared with three in five companies (57%) three years earlier. The use of ethics training had more than doubled to two in five companies (40%), and the use of feedback gathering mechanisms almost doubled to one in two companies (55%).

It was clear that the measures introduced were not as comprehensive (and therefore as effective) as they could be, as the following examples illustrate.

◪ Codes of conduct were not always issued to all employees. By excluding some employees, organisations lose an opportunity to communicate expected standards to those excluded and risk fostering a divisive them-and-us culture.
◪ Few internal stakeholder groups contributed to the development of codes of conduct. This restricted involvement can result in codes that are out of touch with reality and have a negative impact.
◪ Almost half of the companies surveyed that had codes of conduct (45%) did not make them publicly available on request. This represents two missed opportunities: to advertise a commitment to minimum standards of behaviour, and to reinforce this commitment by making them public.
◪ Of the companies providing some form of business ethics training, only three out of five organisations (61%) involved all employees. Not surprisingly, those who receive such training are more likely to be aware of ethical issues.
◪ The content of most training programmes appears to be restricted

to communication of standards and resources such as manuals. The majority of organisations do not cover important areas, such as:
– how standards are applied in practice and what the experience of others in the organisation has been;
– understanding the factors influencing peoples' actions or behaviour and the causes of poor decision-making or unethical conduct.

◪ Stakeholder consultation has increased, and the principal issue now is how far an organisation should go to monitor and address stakeholder impact and how it does it. There is scope for more systematic assessment of activities that may affect stakeholders, so that today's small problems can be identified and prevented from becoming tomorrow's big problems.

◪ Whistle-blowing policies are often flawed in that, for example, they do not protect the whistle-blower's anonymity, thus discouraging people from reporting wrongdoing. However, as a result of the Public Interest Disclosure Act of 1998, UK organisations are at risk if they do not have effective whistle-blowing policies and internal channels through which employees can report wrongdoing.

◪ Feedback gathering mechanisms, such as employee surveys, are conducted by only half of all those surveyed (55%). It is clear that companies could adopt a more systematic approach to gathering feedback. Most of them rely on one method, yet different methods reveal different information. For example, surveys allow broad scanning to provide indications of possible problem areas, whereas focus groups allow in-depth probing of specific areas.

Ethical motivations
The top three factors identified as the main reasons for introducing ethics programmes by more than half of all participants, and which all ranked higher than "new legislation and regulation", are as follows.

1 The desire to protect or improve reputation is the most common factor influencing the development of business ethics activities in organisations, being reported by five out of seven participants (72%).

2 Adherence to corporate governance guidelines, a recurring topic during the last decade, is the second most common factor, being reported by two out of three participants (68%). The publication in 1999 of the Turnbull Report, which emphasised the need for robust internal

controls to manage business risks, is likely to stimulate more activity in this area.

3 In third place came "increased emphasis on values", reported by three out of five participants (58%). This is noteworthy because it signifies recognition by a majority of companies of the importance of values in guiding organisational behaviour.

Ethical pay-off

Overall, the perception of those who have introduced business ethics programmes is that they serve to protect their organisations from significant risks and to some degree help grow the business. Risks such as breaches of law, regulations or company standards and damage to reputation were perceived to be significantly reduced.[3] That business ethics should be a high priority was accepted by the majority of those surveyed. Three in five participants (62%) rated the priority given to business ethics in their organisations as high, compared with one in five (21%) who rated it as low. Those rating the priority high typically described the subject as "fundamental", "essential" or "critical". At the other extreme, the subject was typically regarded as "an overhead" or one that "lacks drive from the top".

Risk awareness

Those lower down the hierarchy – staff and their line managers – are perceived to be least aware of the risks and consequences of unethical behaviour or misconduct. This is not surprising, given their lack of involvement in the creation of codes of conduct and in ethics training. Organisations should develop strategies to increase awareness, especially among line management, to help anticipate and manage these risks.

Global challenges

Over half of those surveyed (57%) had operations in at least three or more of the world's major regions. Many reported ethical concerns, generally around the difficulty of achieving consistent standards (see the example of Nokia) and the issue of corruption.

Protecting their company's reputation is clearly an important priority for those responsible for operations in regions that give rise to such concerns. Many of these concerns surface during informal discussions with colleagues. A genuinely open climate enables such issues to be raised and hopefully tackled before they lead to unexpected consequences. However, companies that use compliance-based approaches cannot be confident that issues will be addressed in time.

Champion importance

Without an effective champion, who has the full support of senior management, a business ethics programme is all too likely to prove ineffectual. Most of the companies surveyed (83%) identified their business ethics champion as an individual at or close to board level. The others identified a department or function, such as internal audit, legal or compliance. A common and important theme is that the role has a good vantage point from which to monitor all business operations and communicate with all parts of the organisation. The role will be marginalised, however, if those at the top do not support it.

Survey conclusions

Many corporate ethics and compliance programmes rely heavily on a code of ethics and a telephone hotline or other formal reporting mechanisms to control employee behaviour. This study suggests, however, that these two mechanisms are the least effective influences on behaviour. Consistency between policies and actions, the rewarding of ethical behaviour and executive leadership's attention to ethics has the greatest impact on controlling employee unethical conduct. Furthermore, the mere existence of a formal mechanism by which ethical wrongdoing can be reported is not enough to encourage such reporting if the behaviour of management and the corporate culture do not support and encourage its use.

Building on the survey

The findings of the UK and US surveys were used to devise a best-practice framework and model. The framework is based on seven pillars of an ethical programme: values, codes, feedback responsibility, training, feedback, reward, external assessment (see Figure 2.2).

Each of the seven components can be improved in terms of designing a best practice programme. For example, there must be consistency between stated organisational values and the behaviour of individuals. There is little point in having a code of ethics that is viewed with cynicism by employees or that is regarded as simply "window-dressing" by external stakeholders. Most companies surveyed did have codes of ethics or conduct. The challenge is to keep the content up-to-date and meaningful. Clearly those companies that involve affected parties in drawing up the code will be at an advantage.

Communication of standards can also be improved. Typically,

Best practice framework

2.2

IDENTIFY	COMMUNICATE		BUILD AND MAINTAIN A RESPONSIBLE DECISION-MAKING CULTURE				
Values/mission statements	Codes of conduct	Feedback gathering and analysis	Functional responsibility	Education and training	Performance reviews/ standards	External assessment
Articulation of what the company stands for	Common framework to guide behaviour	Stakeholder views	In-house expertise	All employees	Setting decision making as well as financial performance measures	Best practice
	Code should emphasise principles over procedures	Surveys/focus groups/ interviews	Leadership	How wrongdoing occurs		Objectivity and independence
Top management consultant		Diagnostics	Corporate Governance needs	Realistic examples	KPIs	Public confidence
Management consistency between values and actions	Developed and supported by both management and staff		Accessible to employees/ management	Sensitivity to diverse employee groups	Rewarding responsible behaviour/ penalising inappropriate behaviour	Verification
			Ownership			

communication of standards takes place at induction. However, the emphasis tends to be on policies and procedures. Best practice indicates that companies should engage employees in more discussion of principles and how these relate to real issues or problems faced in the workplace. More creative forms of communication can also be used such as with the provision of interactive CD-ROMs or video based training. Key messages can also be reinforced through company intranets and other discussion groups.

The remaining cornerstones refer to methods for embedding values into organisational culture. While some companies are gathering the views of employees concerning the company ethics programme this tends to be in rather rudimentary ways. Internal whistle-blowing channels are not likely to be used when there is a lack of confidence in the method of reporting. Best practice indicates that diagnostic tools can be used that are more sophisticated in gaining an understanding of the factors that actually influence unethical conduct.[4]

In the United States there is a more clearly defined functional responsibility for ethics. There are now over 700 members of the Ethics Officer Association. Typically these individuals are not named "ethics officers". However, there is a significant investment in the provision of ethics offices and associated personnel – especially in North America. In Europe and in the UK in particular this role is championed in a less formal way. Best practice indicates that roles need to be integrated into operational decision-making so that ethics is considered as integral to business strategy and operations rather than a bolt-on exercise. Employees need access to key individuals in order to raise issues and seek clarification. More can be done to provide in-house expertise in ethics in this regard.

Business ethics education is rather hit-and-miss. Some companies do invest in ongoing education and training, with simulations and scenarios to keep participants interested. For many companies, though, such education does not make use of real issues that employees encounter. Best practice indicates that realistic examples with sensitivity to the diversity of employee groups can provide more awareness of ethical issues.

Few companies offer performance reviews that include reference to ethical issues. Best practice indicates that the development of key performance indicators relating to ethics is an excellent way of reinforcing and perhaps rewarding ethical conduct. At one extreme performance management and reward systems might actually reinforce unethical conduct. It is crucial, therefore, that companies develop systems that employees have confidence in and that are seen to be working.

Ultimately, increased public and shareholder scrutiny is calling for greater transparency in the approaches that companies are using to manage risk in the workplace. By applying best practice approaches companies will have more confidence that the risk of potential reputation damage is being effectively managed.

Conclusion

Business ethics management is largely about managing the risk to an organisation's reputation, and any risk management programme that does not include a strong emphasis on behaviour is fundamentally flawed. Programme components such as training, reporting systems and feedback-gathering mechanisms must be accompanied by the development of a broader values-based culture that employees see as consistent and believable.

Many organisations grapple with how to make their people "live" their values and codes. Often the key is in the detail – of the design, development, implementation and ongoing maintenance, of all components, not just values and codes. The success of a business ethics programme will ultimately depend on having the right combination of spirit and structure. It will also depend on the cause being championed and supported by senior managers.

3 Integrating ethics into organisational cultures

W. Michael Hoffman, Dawn-Marie Driscoll and
Mollie Painter-Morland

ETHICAL BEHAVIOUR ISN'T AN ACT BUT A HABIT. JUST AS GOOD HEALTH
REQUIRES CULTIVATING THE HABITS OF GETTING ENOUGH SLEEP AND
EATING WHOLESOME FOOD, ARISTOTLE BELIEVED THAT RIGHT ACTION WAS
THE RESULT OF DEVELOPING GOOD MORAL HABITS. IN A BUSINESS
CONTEXT, THIS MEANS TRAINING AND, AT THE DEEPEST LEVEL, SOMETHING
WE CALL "CORPORATE CULTURE."
Jim Kelly, chairman and CEO of United Parcel Post Service

ALTHOUGH ETHICAL MANAGEMENT is being given a higher priority by
many management teams,[1] a wealth of evidence (such as the two
studies in Chapter 2) reveals that managers are still unclear about how to
institute strategies and systems that encourage ethical conduct and help
create a moral corporate culture.[2]

Many managers have opted for the simple route of promulgating rules
and instructing everyone to follow them. Not only is this approach
proving ineffective in today's decentralised business environment, it also
denies employees any chance to become part of the ethical fabric of the
organisation.

Institutional authority versus individual autonomy

The previous chapter made the distinction between compliance
programmes and value-led approaches. This chapter develops these two
concepts, and goes on to argue that the two are not alternatives: both are
essential to encourage ethical behaviour.

Compliance and value-led approaches are the outward manifestation
of two different mindsets that appear to be at war with each other.

Compliance approaches

Compliance programmes are based on a company's belief in its right to
assert its institutional authority. The dictionary says that authority means
the power to command behaviour. Institutional authority:

- defines rules and responsibilities for everyone;
- preserves and unifies core organisational values;
- sets a framework for decision-making.

Compliance programmes work on similar principles, with the goal of "commanding" employees' behaviour. Compliance informs employees about the law and tries to prevent violations. Employees are motivated to do the right thing through the fear of being caught rather than by a desire to be law abiding. Compliance is about obeying rules and authority. Programmes that concentrate only on compliance rarely help employees to resolve situations that are not covered by regulation. Such programmes do not attempt to develop employees' ethical autonomy and responsibility.

Advocates of compliance-based programmes argue that the priority is to teach employees how to meet their legal requirements and to document that the company has complied. In the face of business imperatives, they believe that many employees will forget what they learned in an ethics training course and will do whatever is necessary to get the job done. Many compliance managers feel uncomfortable with words like ethics and values, believing they are too vague and hint at instructing individuals on moral issues.

Value-led approaches
Value-led programmes have their foundations in the individual's right to ethical autonomy. The dictionary defines autonomy as self-directing freedom and independence. In the context of institutions, individual autonomy:

- legitimises the process of appraising and amending organisational policy;
- allows for decentralised decision-making;
- encourages spontaneity and innovation.

Value-driven programmes focus on the company's values and principles and how they apply to situations where no particular rules apply. Employees are helped to become more aware of ethical dilemmas and to make ethically sound decisions. They are also encouraged to ask questions and raise any personal concerns.

Managing the creative tension and interdependence between individual autonomy and institutional authority is the essential challenge of establishing an ethical corporate culture.

From compliance to value-driven: the American journey

The experiences of American companies show why the business ethics movement has moved from a compliance-based approach to one that places emphasis on both compliance and values. Three factors were behind this shift.

1 *Greater liability for all forms of corporate wrongdoing*

The adoption in 1991 of the *Federal Sentencing Guidelines for Organizations* was a significant landmark in the area of corporate accountability and caused company directors to concentrate on minimising the risks of illegal behaviour among employees. The guidelines imposed a system of heavy fines and rigorous probation conditions on organisations convicted of federal crimes.[3] They might have been largely ignored if regulators had not been increasingly fining companies and even sending executives to prison.

Although the guidelines represented a hard stick, they also showed an inviting carrot. Companies that could prove they had implemented an effective system to prevent and detect violations before an offence occurred would be penalised more lightly and could use the establishment of such ethics systems as a defence in civil charges.

The guidelines broke new ground by suggesting what would constitute an effective compliance-based system. This included seven things that an organisation would need to do.

- Establish compliance standards and procedures.
- Assign high-level individuals to oversee compliance.
- Exercise due care in delegating discretionary authority.
- Communicate and train.
- Monitor, audit and provide reliable reporting systems.
- Enforce appropriate discipline with consistency.
- Respond to offences and prevent recurrences.

These were seen as minimum steps. Diligent companies went further in designing their own systems.

Another significant landmark was the Caremark case, decided in 1996. Whereas the sentencing guidelines caught the attention of company lawyers, this case caught the attention of senior managers and boards of directors.[4] Caremark, a medical services company, had been investigated by government regulators for bribing physicians to prescribe Caremark's services. The company and its executives were indicted and eventually paid $250m in fines, reimbursements and penalties. Shareholders alleged that the board of directors breached its fiduciary duty of care to Caremark by failing to supervise employees.

The good news was that the court exonerated the board of directors, finding that the company had established compliance and values reporting systems before the problems began. The bad news was that the court issued a stern warning to other boards, stressing that directors could face liability for failing to have such a programme if improprieties later developed.

Nothing catches the attention of directors more than the word "liable". With the development of the sentencing guidelines (acting as a quasi-best practice model) and the Caremark edict, it is clear that American directors have a legal responsibility to probe, ask questions and establish procedures enabling them to determine the ethical behaviour of employees.

2 The move to self-regulation

Faced with ever tougher penalties, companies realised it was in their best interests to design ethical programmes that went beyond minimum compliance-based standards. Firms looked at ways of both avoiding misconduct and encouraging ethical behaviour.

Ironically, many industry-wide initiatives are based on a model developed as early as 1986 by a group of major defence firms. Called the Defense Industry Initiative on Business Ethics and Conduct (DII), it contained six principles that provided guidance for companies seeking to develop a comprehensive ethics programme.

- Provide a written code of business ethics and conduct.
- Train employees concerning their responsibilities.
- Provide a free and open atmosphere.
- Adopt procedures for voluntary disclosure.
- Be responsible to other companies in the industry.
- Have public accountability.

Industry initiatives are becoming more common. For example, the National Automobile Auction Association, whose members handled $70 billion worth of vehicles in 1997, has adopted a comprehensive code of ethics for all its members, who can be suspended or barred from membership if they violate the code. Following several prominent scandals, the American Council of Life Insurance formulated a voluntary programme of ethical principles and an industry code of conduct. The Chemical Manufacturers Association's Responsible Care Initiative is a voluntary environmental, health and safety performance improvement effort. Member companies, which account for nine-tenths of the country's basic chemical production, pledge to manage their businesses according to the principles set out in the programme, including independent verification.

3 The growth of the business ethics movement and the creation of the new position of ethics officers

Ethics programmes in the United States have evolved from solely emphasising compliance to looking at how to create a moral corporate culture within which individuals can act ethically.

As a result of the DII effort, several large corporations appointed individuals to oversee their compliance efforts. In 1991 the Center for Business Ethics at Bentley College[5] hosted a gathering of approximately 40 ethics managers to share information and common concerns. This meeting led to the formation of the national Ethics Officer Association in 1992. By 2001 its membership had grown to approximately 740 professionals.

Other associations have also formed to help ethics professionals, including The Ombuds Association, the Healthcare Compliance Association and the Office of Government Ethics, which oversees hundreds of ethics and compliance directors within government agencies.

Rules and values: a new alliance

The argument about the relative benefits of compliance programmes compared with values programmes could go on indefinitely, but in truth it begs the wrong question. They are not diverging approaches, but rather complementary components of an ethical programme. Compliance is necessary and many organisations have good compliance programmes in place. The goal is to incorporate them into a value-based management culture. As Frank Daly, corporate director for ethics and business conduct at Northrop Grumman, a defence company, and chairman of the EOA, asserts: "Rules and values are ethical allies."[6]

The key to establishing an ethical culture, which strikes a balance between institutional authority and individual autonomy, is to build an environment that supports personal autonomy while providing proper guidance through codes, rules and policies. The critical task is to develop ethical leadership among all employees and especially to enhance their skills in ethical decision-making. Employees should be encouraged to act as ethical role models and in the process practise ethical leadership skills.

At the Center for Business Ethics, Driscoll and Hoffman designed ten basic steps that companies could take to establish an ethical infrastructure – one that is likely to outlast the tenure of any particular senior manager, and one that will endure in both good and bad economic times.[7]

1 Self-assessment

You cannot plot a course without knowing where you are starting from. A self-assessment, or liability inventory,[8] is a necessary first step to determine what procedures are needed to address organisational risks and concerns. For example, PricewaterhouseCoopers, an international accounting firm, conducted focus group interviews with approximately 400 employees to identify issues that affected them. The firm also reviewed its existing policies before crafting a new policy statement and publishing its code of conduct book, *The Way We Do Business*.

Managers can conduct this in-depth examination themselves, although many prefer to use outside consultants to carry out the survey and analyse the results, much like an auditor's report and letter of recommendation. A comprehensive risk assessment considers what ethical issues have faced competitors and partners, as well as where the company itself has experienced problems. It looks at an organisation's existing compliance efforts and identifies any deficits. Employee surveys and focus groups determine how employees view management and the company; what situations, dilemmas and questions they face; and what might be the underlying cause of future problems. This is sometimes referred to as an ethical climate assessment.

2 Commitment from the top

No ethics initiative should begin without the most senior managers making an explicit commitment to long-term success. Directors should specifically authorise compliance and values programmes and formally appoint a senior officer to oversee them. Many boards require this officer to report to them regularly, usually through the board's audit committee, on progress in implementing the programme. Some boards have established a separate ethics committee of and for the board in addition to its audit committee.

Furthermore, some boards of directors, such as the Michigan Physicians Mutual Liability Company, use board meetings or retreat time to undergo their own customised ethics training, focusing on ethical issues at board level. Consensus about standards of business ethics is critical at this level, one director explained, and must be discussed well before a crisis hits.[9]

Why is it necessary for the board to appoint a senior officer to direct its business conduct programme when it is every employee's responsibility to adhere to company standards and values? The answer is that ethics must be managed like other internal functions. For example, every employee in a company is responsible for financial integrity, but a separate internal auditing group is needed to give this focus and direction and to serve as a check on the process. Ethics managers serve a similar purpose.

Some companies have appointed full-time ethics officers; others underscore the importance of ethical values by giving their chief executive the responsibility. Some do both, like USAA, a diversified financial services company. The chief executive officer, Robert T. Herres, is the chief ethics officer and he appoints an ethics co-ordinator to oversee the programme.

3 Codes of business conduct
A blueprint for building a moral culture within a corporation must include a written code of conduct. These corporate codes of ethics vary in quality and substance. Some consist of a set of specific rules, a list of do's and don'ts. These usually correspond to illegal or unethical actions such as bribery, price-fixing, improper accounting practices and acceptance of gifts. Other codes consist largely of general statements about corporate goals and responsibilities, a kind of credo expressing a company's philosophy and values. The more substantive codes consist of both.

Rules of conduct without a general values statement lack a framework of meaning and purpose; credos without rules of conduct lack specific content.

Olin Corporation

Our Principles of Integrity

◪ Integrity is a fundamental part of Olin's history and the way we do business. Our commitment to integrity means that all of our actions and relationships are based on these uncompromising values:

- ▰ Mutual respect: We treat each other with respect and dignity.
- ▰ Fairness: We deal fairly in all our relationships inside and outside the company.
- ▰ Reliability: We honour our commitments and obligations.
- ▰ Accountability: We take responsibility for our actions.
- ▰ Quality: We deliver safe and reliable products of the highest quality.
- ▰ Opportunity: We provide equal and fair opportunity to all employees.
- ▰ Compliance: We comply with all laws and regulations
- ▰ Honesty: We always tell the truth at Olin.
- ▰ Community: We positively contribute to the community.

Furthermore, codes of conduct should not imply that whatever has not been strictly prohibited is thereby allowed. A code cannot list and mandate every form of ethical or unethical conduct, nor should it try to. Business ethics, like all areas of ethics, has grey areas that require individual discretion and thought. A good corporate code of values and conduct should include certain managerial and employee guidelines for making ethical decisions, including the principles and factors that ought to be considered before arriving at a decision.[10]

Comprehensive codes should also include sources of advice and counsel available inside and outside the corporation, as well as real examples from the company's experience or industry that help illustrate a potential ethical dilemma. Whatever these guidelines include, they should make people aware that they might need to make difficult ethical judgments based on a code's implicit values, rather than on the letter of the law. Employees should also know that they are accountable for their behaviour. This will give them a greater sense of personal ethical responsibility and send a clear message that corporate integrity is dependent on individual integrity.

Organisations that begin an ethics initiative with written codes often discover that many employees do not read them, even when the document is put in front of them. Frank Daly of Northrop Grumman has a good suggestion: codes of conduct should be policies that are easy to read and easily understood by people who don't like to read, can't read or respond much better to visual information. Take creative licence in the presentation.

Some companies with mature ethics programmes have reduced voluminous codes of conduct to just a few core values, trusting that their employees will do the right thing when confronted with a situation that poses no easy answers.

Identifying the core values

Texas Instruments, a global semiconductor company, had a distinguished reputation for ethics, winning prestigious national awards for its programme in 1991 and 1994. In 1997 it embarked on a massive effort to eliminate rules and policies and distil its voluminous policy book to a short codification of the company's core values. After months of focus groups, consultation and drafts, the company ended up with just three words: integrity, innovation and commitment.

4 Communication vehicles

The best ethics programme in the world is worth little if it is not communicated well, in various forms and frequently. In this respect, companies can learn from what others are doing.

BellSouth, a telecommunications company, uses a variety of ways of communicating its ethical standpoint, *A Commitment to Our Personal Responsibility*. Duane Ackerman, president and chief executive officer, introduced the programme by sending a letter to every employee. Each also received an attractive 40-page booklet containing BellSouth's code of conduct, information on over 20 different subjects (including the law, BellSouth's policies and sample questions and answers) and a resource guide for further questions. Employees were given a wallet-sized card with the toll-free telephone number of the ethics line. All supervisors held meetings with employees to discuss ethical concerns. Employees viewed dramatisations of ethical dilemmas in a training video and discussed them with the ethics officer and several BellSouth supervisors. At the end of the training, every employee signed a statement indicating they had read and understood the information provided.

Employees can submit questions anonymously to the ethics office via the company's website or through their own company e-mail address. They are encouraged to call the company's human resources department, the legal department, the security department, the auditing department or the ethics office if they need information and guidance.

BellSouth's ethics officer, Jerry Guthrie, constantly communicates the values and ethics message of the company, inviting himself to departmental meetings, gatherings of company lawyers, human resource managers and even conferences of the company's international managers. Finding new and effective ways to communicate company values is one of his top priorities.

5 Training

Communication alone is not sufficient to convert values into action. Employees may think they know how to make an ethical decision, but they may not know how to think through the process of evaluating potential courses of action and their consequences, or understand what the organisation would like them to do in difficult circumstances. This is particularly true when employees come from diverse backgrounds, cultures and life experiences. A programme of ethics training is crucial, and to be most effective it should allow employees to exchange views with each other about the importance of ethics and about compliance and values that specifically relate to their daily work. Weaknesses of training programmes include:

- being too brief to accomplish anything significant;
- inadequately preparing participants in advance of the session;
- failing to consider the larger context of an overall corporate ethics development effort.

Some good ethics training sessions are delivered online, enabling employees to take the interactive courses individually and spend as much time as they need reviewing various topics.

At the very least, ethics training should:

- clarify the ethical values and enhance the ethical awareness of employees;
- uncover and investigate ethical issues and concerns that directly relate to the organisation;
- discuss criteria for ethical decision-making within the organisation;
- examine and enrich the structures, strategies, resources, policies and goals that shape the ethical environment and guide the ethical activities of the organisation.

Ethics training should help participants see or recognise ethical issues, especially those that are not self-evident. An effective session should fit the participants with "moral lenses" through which they will see their world from an ethical point of view.

6 Resources for assistance

In the early stages of the business ethics movement, companies set up free telephone hotlines as a way for employees to report wrongdoing. But as the calls came in, managers realised that employees were not necessarily reporting actual illegalities and that it was difficult for all concerned to discern whether a particular set of facts constituted a violation of law. Managers saw the value of repositioning these hotlines as "helplines" or "guidelines", providing employees with advice and counsel on ethical and compliance issues.

Some companies choose to rely on an open-door policy and a clear code of conduct as a means of encouraging employees to report wrongdoing. But some employees are sceptical about open-door systems that require subordinates to confront their boss or their boss's boss. They prefer anonymous calls instead. Although some companies staff hotlines with their own personnel, a significant number have turned to outside professional services, which provide 24-hour-a-day, 365-days-a-year coverage.

These helplines have not become vehicles for cynical or revengeful whistle-blowers with false information, as some feared. Companies such as Lockheed Martin have implemented procedures that reduce the number of false accusations without impairing the efficacy of the ethics hotline. Callers are asked to state their name, but this information is not included in any further documentation. In most cases, the caller's identity is known only to the ethics officer, as a form of corporate "witness protection".

Monitoring ethical misconduct

Lockheed Martin's Ethics and Business Conduct Steering Committee reviewed statistics about ethical misconduct across the company, showing that in one 15-month period, approximately 70 Lockheed Martin employees were discharged and another 70 suspended for ethical lapses. Furthermore, more than 450 employees received some other type of sanction during the same period. As Lockheed Martin itself said, these were good employees who, for a variety of reasons, made bad ethical choices.

The reasons, all too familiar to any organisation, included pressure to meet a deadline or goal, lack of resources, peer pressure, or a belief that the decision was in the organisation's best interest.

At Northrop Grumman, *When to Challenge* guidelines are an important part of its value statement. Employees are told that if they are ever asked to do something that they believe is either unethical or not in the company's best interest, or if they become aware of any such activities, it is their right and their responsibility to express their concerns. The advantage of a clear statement and guideline like Northrop Grumman's is that it answers perhaps the most difficult ethical questions for an employee: Is whistle-blowing morally obligatory? Must we take action to prevent harm as well as not cause it ourselves?

Companies with extensive resources for assistance, from telephone lines to websites to ethics offices and e-mail, make it easy for their employees to make difficult ethical choices according to the company's values.[11]

7 *Organisational ownership*

No ethics officer is an island and no programme to put ethics into action will be successful without the full involvement of employees across the organisation. For that reason, multidepartmental committees effectively support any ethics initiative. With managers drawn from diverse departments across the company (human resources, security, legal and auditing being crucial), the ethics officer has a "kitchen cabinet" to serve as a sounding board and to drive ownership of the programme throughout all areas of the business. The committee also helps utilise the resources available in participating departments.

At USAA, for example, the ethics co-ordinator is part of the CEO's office and works closely with the company's Ethics Council, a group of senior executives who review issues of major significance and take appropriate action. The council comprises the senior vice-president and chief financial officer, who chairs the group, the senior vice-president, general counsel and corporate secretary, the president of the USAA Alliance Services Company and the president of the USAA Life Insurance Company.

One risk of a corporate-directed ethics initiative is that it will not take hold in the outlying areas and locations. To prevent this, some companies have made specific field managers responsible for implementing ethics initiatives in their area. Depending on the industry, some companies have assigned responsibility for discrete risk areas to an individual, who then supplies other employees with expert advice. These "responsible officers" develop an expertise in certain high-risk areas, such as environmental compliance, and may join a team containing a lawyer and the manager responsible for ethical initiatives in a particular area.[12]

8 Consistent response and enforcement

Some ethics officers have admitted that implementing an ethics programme consistently is one of their toughest challenges, especially in organisations with thousands of employees located at many different sites. The most effective way to undercut an ethics programme is to discipline a low-level employee or one who is not well liked, while ignoring similar wrongdoings by a senior executive or star performer. Companies can ensure consistent enforcement by carefully co-ordinating with human resources personnel or by establishing an ethics co-ordinating committee that can review or hear appeals on disciplinary actions.

A consistent response to ethical issues involves more than tackling wrongdoing. Some organisations have built-in incentives, evaluations and rewards for employees who demonstrate ethical character, understanding that an employee can diligently follow all procedures but still be viewed as a person with questionable values. Shirley Peterson, former corporate vice-president of organisation development and ethics at Northrop Grumman, helped the company implement its Leadership Inventory, a checklist of behavioural characteristics tied directly to Northrop values. Managers receive a summary of how others evaluated them which identifies any aspects of their behaviour that they need to change.[13] This process ensures that Northrop's performance appraisal systems are well integrated with its values mission and that both good and bad behaviour are treated uniformly.

9 Audits and measurements

Managers should not establish ethics initiatives, training programmes and other infrastructure without constantly measuring their effectiveness. On the process side, audits should reveal whether communication vehicles such as helplines or websites are working and whether employees have acknowledged receiving training and are aware of available resources. Substantive audits should include detailed investigations into potential violations of law or regulation.

Many companies already carry out compliance audit and monitoring by listening to the way telephone representatives impart information, and by reviewing advertisements, documents or bid processes. Auditing how employees adhere to an organisation's values is more difficult, but many companies are finding effective ways to judge whether their programmes are working. They use employee, customer and supplier satisfaction surveys, focus groups and detailed exit interviews, often conducted by outside consultants, to glean unbiased feedback.

If executives are serious about implementing ethical management, they should be equally serious about evaluating how well their programmes are succeeding. Carrie Penman, deputy director of the Ethics Officer Association and former ethics officer at Westinghouse, a diversified conglomerate, said:

> Everyone's struggling with audits and measurements. Most ethics officers track helpline calls, but that usually doesn't cut it when the board asks them to measure adherence to company values. I'd like an approach that is detailed yet practical, but it may be difficult to design something that will be applicable to a wide range of organisations and industries. I'm not sure one size fits all.

Penman's experience at Westinghouse has given her an appreciation for non-quantifiable measurements.

> I trust my gut instinct. At Westinghouse, I answered my phone myself. I could tell you which locations called most often and which ones I never heard from. I could tell you which locations and managers had problems, and which were the most responsive to what we were trying to do. I could hear tones of frustration or anger from callers from certain areas of the company, and I could tell the difference in the attitude of various managers when I tried to resolve an issue with them.
>
> As I developed more confidence in my gut instinct, just by doing my job day to day, I could say to our auditor, "Here's where you ought to go and check". I would pay as much attention to what I was not hearing as to where the calls were coming from. A lot of my auditing came down to assessing management style. If I suspected managers were

> *telling their employees, "Don't tell me your problems, just*
> *get the job done", I knew it would invariably indicate bigger*
> *problems.*

10 Revision and refinements

Values programmes must be allowed to evolve. Every month, every year, circumstances and situations change, requiring managers to re-evaluate the goals and content of their programmes. At Motorola, for example, the ethics initiative is called *Motorola Ethics Renewal Process*. In an attempt to be flexible and meaningful for the company's 150,000 employees, 60% of whom work outside the United States, the emphasis is on the word "process". Rather than using a formal programme or a detailed audit, Motorola managers have tried to meet their goal of being the most trusted company in the world by giving employees a process to discuss tough issues.[14]

Revising the code

Guardsmark, an American private security company, adopted its first ethics code in 1980 and had revised it three times by 1990. In 1991, however, Guardsmark's chairman, Ira Lipman, decided that the code should be revised every year. The company now embarks on a comprehensive process each year, soliciting suggestions from its 14,000 employees. In 1999, for example, the company received 304 employee suggestions for changes. Every September the previous code of ethics expires and the new, revised, improved code is signed and adopted by every employee in the company.

Companies are always in danger of being caught by shifting sands unless they carefully monitor regulatory changes and new developments in their industry. This naturally requires them to revise their own operations. There are numerous examples of behaviour and practices that were tolerated, or even encouraged, one month and then considered to be on the wrong side of the line a month later. For example, when the Securities and Exchange Commission's chairman, Arthur Levitt, gave a speech in September 1998 attacking what he considered bad financial reporting, alert certified public accountants, finance officers and others took notice. Now what might have been considered as accounting irregularities could well be regarded as financial fraud. The difference is not minor.

Sometimes managers feel that if a procedure or practice has been initiated in the name of ethics or compliance, it is untouchable. This is not so. Sometimes a fresh look is needed, as well as a courageous hand to stop the continuation of an idea whose time has passed.

Sometimes revision and reform comes about because an organisation discovers that an ethical principle or value it had held as sacrosanct has become the subject of debate and divisiveness. Of course, managers should never cave in to those who shout the loudest, but raised voices sometimes give a clue that change is needed.

The European experience

Various models of corporate governance co-exist in Europe. Nevertheless the European economic landscape has been changing rapidly and the European Union is looking to support the development of responsible business practices. For example, a new EU directive on corporate social responsibility (CSR) is being considered that would force pension funds to disclose their socially responsible investment (SRI) policies. And 2005 has been announced by the EU as European year on corporate social responsibility. These and other developments indicate that there is both pressure and support for companies taking an active stance on ethical issues.

The launch is expected in 2001 of the European Business Ethics Network – Forum for Ethics Practitioners (FEP), the European equivalent of the Ethics Officer Association (EOA) in the United States. The forum will provide opportunities for the numerous ethics practitioners who already meet around Europe to share experiences and best practice knowledge. The experience of ethics officers in the United States will be invaluable for those with equivalent roles in Europe. However, the emphasis has been more on the softer side of regulation than some of the punitive measures in the United States. Whatever the motivation to move towards a fuller consideration of ethical business practices, on both sides of the pond there is a need to obtain the right balance between compliance and values.

Conclusion

When Peter Drucker, a famous management guru, was 13 a teacher asked him what he wanted to be remembered for. Drucker, now over 80 and still a prolific writer, is still trying to answer that question, "because it pushes you to see yourself as a different person – the person you can become".[15]

So it is with ethics and organisational cultures. Developing an organisational ethical culture is a continuous process, not something that reaches completion. Bill Davis, CEO and chairman of Niagara Mohawk Holdings, a major New York public utilities company, captured this when talking about his company's award-winning ethics programme:[16]

> *There is no end to this game. You never cross the goal line and you can't run out the clock. You have to keep up the effort, even when things seem to be going well.*

2

INDIVIDUALS AND ORGANISATIONS

4 Ethical fitness in today's business environment

Rushworth Kidder and Sheila Bloom

IN THE TWENTY-FIRST CENTURY, SURVIVAL WILL BE A MORE COMPLICATED
AND PRECARIOUS QUESTION THAN EVER BEFORE, AND THE ETHICS
REQUIRED OF US MUST BE CORRESPONDINGLY SOPHISTICATED.
>Oscar Arias, former president of Costa Rica and winner of the
>1987 Nobel Peace Prize

IT BEGAN as a simple request. As chief legal officer, Alistair was asked by his board of directors to look into rumours of price-fixing in the company's continental operations.

Alistair's firm specialised in producing low-cost medical kits for use in developing countries, refugee areas and combat zones. It also operated in high-end international markets, where competition was fierce. Alistair took his assignment seriously. His firm had a long-standing commitment to ethical business practice. His directors especially opposed price-fixing, bribery and kickbacks.

The price-fixing rumours proved groundless, but Alistair kept hearing whispers about "the Bosnia contract". A global relief organisation had underwritten the distribution of a million kits in some of the most conflicted regions of Bosnia. Like most such contracts with charitable organisations, it contained hardly any profit for his firm. What's more, the contract looked ordinary except for a large commission to a Romanian distributor. Seeking out the person in his own firm who had negotiated the contract, Alistair had one question in mind: was this a bribe?

Yes and no, was the reply. The Romanian distributor had said that local militia units regularly set up roadblocks throughout Bosnia and demanded money from the drivers distributing the kits. Drivers without cash had been taken from their trucks and shot. If the kits were to be delivered, it was argued, this was a cost of doing business.

Alistair felt sure that none of the money had flowed back to the person who negotiated the contract, whose only motive was to get the kits delivered. By this time, the contract was completed. Yet Alistair still faced a dilemma. Should he let the matter rest or should he inform the board?

Weighing the options, Alistair felt that this kind of activity was not in the firm's long-term interests. Everything in his background told him this was not the way to do business. Bribery was unacceptable to the directors, who felt strongly that once this barrier was breached there would be no stopping future shakedowns. Alistair agreed in principle. In everything he did, at work and with his family, he tried to hold to principles that he felt ought to be universal, generally applied and fair. "Don't give bribes" was certainly one of them.

But as a compassionate individual, Alistair also felt that it was vital to provide medicine for the wounded. Yes, he could stick to his principles – and people would die because the trucks would never get through. Besides, this was a war zone, where the normal ethic of commerce could not be so easily applied. The medicine could have been delivered using other methods, but these would almost certainly have caused delays that might have meant the difference between life and death for innocent sufferers. The Bosnia contract had not been ideal but it had accomplished much good for many people.

What should Alistair do? What would you do?

These questions force us to come to terms with one of the toughest challenges facing managers today: ethical dilemmas in which both sides are "right". The usual definition of ethics – that it is a matter of right versus wrong – is not much help. Alistair had done no wrong, yet he still faced an ethical dilemma. The colloquial description of "grey areas" doesn't help. Alistair was not facing a woolly, fuzzy issue. There were powerful moral arguments on each side, clearly identified in black-and-white terms. The issue permitted no greyness: either you bribed or you did not, people either died or lived, and you reported or kept quiet.

Ethical fitness: a four-step workout

Alistair knew that he faced a difficult dilemma. But he also had a quality not universally found in today's business culture, something we call "ethical fitness". He was in shape to spot and respond to moral issues and prepared to flex his thinking when encountering new challenges. Ethical conundrums did not frighten him, any more than a hard workout scares an athlete. Alistair's ethical fitness had been built up over time, through steady mental exercise. He had stayed in shape by running to meet moral issues rather than fleeing from the encounter.

From their experiences and research the authors have concluded that ethical fitness develops through a four-step, reiterative process.

◪ **Step 1 Moral awareness:** a sensitivity to emerging ethical issues and a willingness to see their broad implications. This awareness helps create conditions of trust enabling people to deal with issues and to read the moral barometer astutely and accurately.

◪ **Step 2 Values definition:** discovering and articulating the core, cross-cultural, shared moral values underlying any ethical activity, regardless of culture or geographical location.

◪ **Step 3 Ethical analysis:** identifying and categorising various paradigms for right-versus-right dilemmas facing individuals and institutions in business and elsewhere.

◪ **Step 4 Dilemma resolution:** applying a set of principles to arrive at a reasoned, acceptable, defensible choice between the two right courses of action posed by an ethical dilemma.

The rest of this chapter explores these four elements of ethical fitness and applies them to the present-day global business culture.[1]

Moral awareness

Moral lapses occur when individuals fail to grasp the ethical implications of a situation. The moral concerns go right past them. They never even see there might be a problem. Nothing is more important for fostering an ethical business climate than this: to improve the moral awareness of individual managers, so that they see ethical dilemmas as they approach not after they have struck.

Moral awareness involves three things: significance, trust and reading the moral barometer.

Significance

This is the recognition that ethics matter, deeply and inescapably, to our common global future. The meltdown at Chernobyl, the explosion of the Challenger spacecraft, the grounding of the Exxon Valdez and the collapse of Barings bank all have common elements. Each involved an individual or a small handful of people making manifestly unethical decisions. Each employed complex, cutting-edge technologies – nuclear reactors, space vehicles, ocean-going tankers and financial systems – and computer-based structures that rapidly amplified these small unethical decisions into situations of enormous consequence. The technology leveraged the ethics – what began as small unethical choices exploded into world-class disasters.

As technological leveraging increases, the ability to make sound ethical decisions becomes exponentially more important. A century ago, a Ukrainian power-plant operator, an American engineer designing O-rings, a ship's captain, or a 29-year-old English trader could not have produced global disasters at such speed. The fact that such catastrophes can happen today, triggered not by the managing director or the chairman but by managers and staff working deep within an organisation, suggests the importance of ethics throughout an entire business.

It is tempting to think that moral problems can be solved by improving the analytical skills of employees. The evidence argues otherwise. The individuals involved in the situations cited above were all very smart. They were not lacking rational acumen, but rather the conscience and character to apply it for ethical ends. It may not be enough for us to be as ethical as our ancestors were. The demands of survival may require us to be far more ethical simply because, with today's technologies, the stakes are far higher. As technology spreads access to information in more democratic ways – allowing children, hackers and criminals equal entry to World Wide Web – it will no longer be enough to require sound ethics only at the top, among the gatekeepers. What will these keepers do when there are no longer any gates?

Trust

If ethics are to be applied to the ongoing rough-and-tumble of our individual and corporate lives, we need to create conditions of trust. The *Oxford English Dictionary* defines trust as "confidence in or reliance on some quality or attribute of a person or thing, or the truth of a statement". It involves both trustfulness (a sense of confidence in others) and trustworthiness (whereby an individual acts so as to engender trust and be worthy of the confidence of others).

In today's business context, trust almost always means trustworthiness – inspiring customers, vendors, regulators, the media and the public to feel confident in and rely on a person, team, organisation, product or service. But how do you create trustworthiness? One of the best ways is to act with trustfulness – since trusting others encourages them to trust you. This reciprocity is suggested by the adjective "mutual", so often applied to trust. "Trust inevitably requires some sense of mutuality, or reciprocal loyalty," writes Charles Handy, a British business author and philosopher.[2] Or as John Dalla Costa, a Canadian author, puts it: "Dignity extended to employees and customers by the company creates the foundation for trust to be exchanged."[3]

Current business literature unhesitatingly identifies trust as a key factor in successful leadership and management. Robert Levering, co-author of *The 100 Best Companies to Work for in America*, identifies trust as one of the three key elements in his "best company" formula. He writes:

> *A great place to work is one where you trust the people you work for, have pride in what you do, and enjoy the people you work with."*[4]

By contrast, lack of trust in a business context is seen as crucially debilitating. Manfred Kets de Vries of INSEAD, a French business school, writes:

> *If there is no sense of trust in the organisation, if people are preoccupied with protecting their backs, creativity will be one of the first casualties.*[5]

In a global corporate arena, where individuals are working together in virtual relationships, lack of trust is fatal. As organisations grow more multinational and disparate, no manager can constantly oversee every relationship. Management is becoming a virtual process. "How do you manage people whom you do not see?" asks Handy. His simple answer is: "By trusting them."[6] Building on the idea of reciprocity, he argues:

> *A lack of trust makes employees untrustworthy [which] does not bode well for the future of virtuality in organisations. If we are to enjoy the efficiencies and other benefits of the virtual organisation, we will have to rediscover how to run organisations based more on trust than on control.*[7]

Probing these ideas further in *Trust: The Social Virtues and the Creation of Prosperity*, Francis Fukuyama, a social scientist and public policy professor, applies the relationship between trust and ethics beyond business to the entire range of social capital. For him, trust is not merely a "soft" concept, but something inextricably wedded to bottom-line performance. He argues:

> *If people ... trust one another because they are all operating according to a common set of ethical norms, doing business costs less.*[8]

Reading the moral barometer

This is the ability to chart the ethical trend-lines, both those that point towards moral debasement and those that suggest rising moral probity, and then try to assess their relative weight and get a sense of where the curve is heading.

The moral barometer helps to answer the age-old question of moral philosophy: "Are we getting better or worse?" The point is not to assign some mathematical measure to the trend-lines, nor to decide absolutely whether ethics is declining or improving. Instead, it is to heighten people's moral awareness by helping them recognise that ethics is a continuous influence that affects everyone. Being alert to these developments goes a long way towards building ethical fitness.

Core shared values

Implicit in this discussion of moral awareness is a sense of values. Assigning "rising" and "falling" categories to behaviour suggests a metric, a set of standards measuring the morality of an issue or event. But what guarantee is there that those values are not simply personal, individually derived and unique to us? Do we hold values in common or are your judgments unique to you and mine to me?

Research at the Institute for Global Ethics (IGE) over the past decade strongly indicates the presence of a common core of shared, global values operating in the ethical realm. In a study of shared values, 24 ethical exemplars from 16 nations identified the values they would include in a global code of ethics for the 21st century. Among scores of values, eight were ranked so highly that they appeared universal: love, truth, freedom, fairness, unity, tolerance, responsibility and respect for life.[9]

Since 1992 over 10,000 people have gone through the IGE's Ethical Fitness™ Seminar, mostly in the United States but increasingly around the world. One exercise asks participants to identify the five most important moral values they would like to carve above the door of a new school. With uncanny regularity participants identify five values – compassion, honesty, fairness, respect and responsibility – that strongly echo those in the shared values study mentioned above.

In an IGE survey conducted in 1996 at the State of the World Forum in San Francisco, 272 participants from 40 countries and 50 distinct faith groups identified a set of values that began with truth (169 votes), compassion (153) and responsibility (147). Respondents also put respect and fairness high on the list. The survey showed no significant statistical differences between males and females, native English and non-native English speakers, or among individuals of different faith groups. Most important, perhaps, were responses to a question asking participants to put themselves on a scale from "deeply religious" to "not religious at all". There were no statistically significant differences across that scale. Those with no religious leanings identified the same moral values as those who considered themselves deeply religious.

These studies suggest that people's core moral values are very deep, transcending not only cultures and gender but religion as well. They invite the hypothesis that all over the world there are individuals committed to the same broad values. Although they may express them in different ways, put them in different hierarchies and even attach somewhat different meanings to the terms, there exists a core of values that is universal, deeply embedded, and probably enduring.

Side-stepping Hobson

The impact of this finding for the global business community cannot be overstated. A principal impediment to establishing global ethical standards in multinational businesses lies in the perception that to do so raises Hobson's choice. Multinational executives face two possible options. They can say: "We have clear values here at headquarters, and we intend to impose them upon every business unit around the world, whether they like it or not." Alternatively, they can say: "Every culture is different, so we must not condemn behaviours in our far-flung business units that we would consider unethical and even illegal."

Neither stance is viable. An ethics programme without consistent standards and values is not an ethics programme. Yet if, as Lord Moulton of Bank once argued, ethics is "obedience to the unenforceable" whereas law is "obedience to the enforceable", then any effort to impose ethics degenerates into mere regulation.[10] This subverts the power of the ethical impulse and encourages resistance among those upon whom it is imposed.

The second stance rests on the belief that societies everywhere have their own sets of cultural, social and business values. So they do. Fortunately, however, they also share a core set of moral values prized by many other traditions, religions and ethnic groups. This makes it possible to disarm Hobson of his choice. Common moral values do not need to be imposed because they already exist. An ethics programme built on such values can have global resonance and local relevance. It can be used to inform, and sometimes challenge, any business and social values that seem to run as cross-currents to the ethical values.

Values provide a commonality that binds an organisation together in pursuit of a common ethic. They provide the groundwork for a successful ethics programme. Fortunately, corporate executives increasingly recognise these facts. As the previous chapter argued, the late 1990s saw a strong move within corporations from compliance-based to values-based ethics programmes. And there is a wealth of evidence in Chapter 2 to show that values are in the ascendancy and emphasise that a shared understanding of the way a company wishes to conduct business is more important than the existence of formal statements.[11]

Ethical analysis

If shared understanding is more important than formal statements, then how do organisations embed their core values in such a way as to elevate understanding over formalism? The answer is to bring the capacity for ethical fitness to the desktops of individual managers. This capacity begins with the recognition of the relationship between core values and ethical dilemmas. Given the existence of these shared values, it is clear that ethical issues arise for one of two reasons.

- Departure from core ethical values. If honesty is a core value, dishonest actions violate that value and are manifestly unethical. Such actions represent right-versus-wrong issues, or moral temptations.
- Conflict between two core values. A person experiences great ethical tension because two of his or her deeply held values are pitted against each other. Such actions represent right-versus-right issues, or ethical dilemmas.

There are a great number of right-versus-wrong moral temptations in the modern global business environment. Through heightened moral awareness, managers can understand the dangers, both personal and organisational, of unethical action. An understanding of core values helps because they provide a clear metric for defining unethical behaviour. After all, if ethics consists in adhering to honesty, compassion, fairness, responsibility and respect, then unethical behaviour is that which is dishonest, lacking in compassion, unfair, irresponsible or disrespectful.

In practice, however, the toughest ethical issues are not right versus wrong. Once people define side A as right, good and noble and side B as wrong, perverse and foul, they do not usually say: "And here I stand, stuck in the middle, unable to decide what to do." Useful ethics training equips managers to probe such situations until seemingly obscure moral questions become stark polarities of right and wrong, enabling them to make the right choice without great anguish.

Right-versus-right issues are far tougher. When both sides have a strong claim to the moral high ground, how are managers to choose? These are the really tough decisions. In Alistair's case, for example, two powerful core values come into conflict: his high standard of fairness versus his deep feeling of compassion. The decision can be argued nobly on either side, but it cannot be resolved by doing both things. A choice must be made. These sorts of dilemmas are usually more wrenching and subtler than right-versus-wrong moral temptations. In today's society, they are also more commonplace.

Right-versus-right dilemmas: the four types

Alistair's choice illustrates one of four patterns, into which the IGE research suggests that right-versus-right dilemmas fall: a *justice versus mercy* paradigm.[12] Three other dilemma paradigms provide equally powerful drivers for our toughest choices: *truth versus loyalty, short-term versus long-term* and *individual versus community*. Here are illustrations of each, based on real-life experiences described to the authors by executives who witnessed them.

JUSTICE VERSUS MERCY

On the justice side, otherwise called fairness, equity or principle, is the demand for adherence to standards, norms, rules and accepted practices. It argues for consistency of application, universality in approach and commonality across a variety of cases. It depends on established expectations, and builds a powerful moral case for adhering to them.

But mercy, which could also be called compassion, love or caring, calls instead for an exception to the rule. Arguing the formidable moral case for the dignity and needs of the often-suffering individual, it insists on doing what is best for the person involved in this case, without necessarily worrying about precedent or appearance. Should a manager overlook a glaring, costly error by a subordinate whose son has suddenly been admitted to hospital? Justice argues one side and mercy the other, and both are right.

TRUTH VERSUS LOYALTY

When Alan arrived for his weekly mentoring session with Sarah, an external senior consultant, he was in a state of high excitement. He and his wife had made a successful offer for the house of their dreams. The house was expensive, but their mortgage lender was willing to finance 95% of the cost because Alan had gained a significant promotion and salary increase six months earlier.

Alan's company had assigned him an external mentor to help him adjust to his new position. Sarah and he had formed a close working relationship, so that she knew about his financial situation and his personal aspirations. Sarah also knew that Alan's wife had put her own career on hold to bring up their two small children and that the family depended on Alan's earnings alone.

But Sarah knew something else. She had also been engaged by Alan's firm to advise on the general impact of amalgamating two major departments, one of which was Alan's. The newly restructured department would not require three managers. It was probable that Alan, as the least experienced of the three, would lose his job.

Sarah found herself in a difficult position. On the one hand, she knew that Alan had placed great trust in her by sharing confidential information about his life. Furthermore, the mentoring programme depended on openness, honesty, and truth-telling on both sides, qualities that had been present throughout their relationship. On the other hand, Sarah was bound by an equally strong loyalty to her employers to hold in strictest confidence everything she knew about the restructuring.

Sarah had done nothing wrong yet she faced a wrenching ethical dilemma, not because she lacked values but precisely because two of her core values – truth and loyalty – were coming into direct conflict. What should she do?

INDIVIDUAL VERSUS COMMUNITY

Nigel, the managing director of a small, successful manufacturing firm, was at home one Saturday afternoon some years ago when he heard a piece of news that was destined to plunge him into a serious right-versus-right dilemma. John, one of his employees, had been in a minor automobile accident that had left him bleeding. When the paramedics arrived, John asked them to glove up, as he was HIV positive. This was in the mid-1980s, when panic and misinformation about AIDS was at its worst in Europe and America.

The ambulance men were untrained and they panicked. A local reporter appeared on the scene, and photographs subsequently appeared in the local press showing the paramedics burning their uniforms in the street. Visible in the background was John's car, with its number plate clearly legible.

It didn't take long for the story to spread. Although John was a popular and respected employee, word got round by Monday morning that he was HIV positive. Following a quickly convened meeting, the shop-floor employees decided that they could not work with John and would strike if he remained in employment.

In those fast-moving few hours, Nigel also got a call from the chief executive of his firm's major customer. Clearly, that executive didn't want a strike as his firm depended on supplies from Nigel's firm. But given the nature of the business (the production of food products), neither did he want his company's brand name linked to an individual who was HIV positive, in case there was a health risk which could be transmitted to consumers (a fear subsequently proved to be erroneous). Yet he was uneasy about being blamed in any way for the termination of an employee who was otherwise healthy and hard working.

Nigel needed to act fast. On one hand, it was right to treat John with compassion, dignity and fairness. On the other hand, the community of employees and managers in both firms needed to be protected from threats to health, safety, morale and reputation that, in the absence of any clear medical or scientific guidelines, were understandably frightening and perplexing. By sacrificing one individual, Nigel could restore order and calm. But weren't individual rights supremely important, constituting the only basis, in fact, upon which an effective community could be sustained? What should Nigel do?

SHORT-TERM VERSUS LONG-TERM

Janet, a senior executive, worked for a major Los Angeles-based multinational, which encouraged its executives to serve in charitable capacities. Janet had followed her keen interest in education and had been a trustee for 15 years of a non-profit organisation created to supply science-related educational materials to teachers and schools. Janet and the other trustees had recently taken the decision to spin off part of the organisation's activities into a for-profit corporation. This would provide a secure revenue stream for the organisation, which was on slightly shaky financial ground. If all went well, and if private investors remained committed to purchasing shares in the newly created entity, the deal should be closed within six months.

At the next board meeting, however, Janet learned that Ben, the organisation's chief financial officer, had been caught stealing from it. Janet liked Ben very much. Although he was not a trustee, he had been a fixture at their meetings for several years and was affable, competent and engaged. Now an unusually thorough audit had revealed that over four years Ben had skimmed about $185,000 from the organisation, using the money to help cover payments on a new and expensive house.

So far, the police had not been brought in. No charges had been filed. A repentant Ben agreed to resign and repay the money he had stolen. But the board was split on how it should respond.

One faction insisted that the matter remain under wraps. Given the complexity of the spin-off, and the importance of its success to the long-term prosperity of the parent organisation, they argued that public exposure would scare off investors. Although the issue was serious, it was not a mortal blow to the non-profit organisation. It would probably have no real bearing on the new for-profit company. Besides, Ben had put in several years of otherwise good service. He had promised to repay the money. Yes, he had made a series of decisions that were wholly dishonest. But as a modestly paid employee trying to raise a family in one of America's most expensive housing markets, his lapse was understandable, even if unforgivable. The best decision would be to respect the organisation's short-term, vital need for a successful spin-off and keep quiet about Ben.

Other trustees had an entirely different view. Ben, they insisted, should be punished to the full extent of the law – not simply to make an example, but to make sure that no other organisation would find itself his unwitting victim in the future. Yes, this choice would make life more difficult in the short term – and could even make the spin-off impossible. But in the long term, they could not live with themselves as members of the charitable sector if they allowed Ben's blight to spread to other organisations.

These trustees also argued that the news would eventually get out. Would the investors in the for-profit begin to question the value of the company Ben had helped create? Would they suspect that the financial picture they had been given of the new firm was as dishonest as the finance officer who had painted it? If the new company ran into financial problems, would unhappy investors sue the non-profit parent for concealing an important fact about a man so instrumental to the deal? As unpleasant as it was, they argued, it would be best to take the hit in the short term by making everything public.

Janet's was the swing vote. What should she do?

Resolving tough dilemmas

Why it is important to identify the ethical paradigms? There are three reasons.

- ◪ It helps to demystify the process, moving ethics from the realm of the obtuse, bizarre or "touchy-feely" into the range of analytical structures, critical thinking and rational understanding.
- ◪ It helps us to understand why the issue we face seems so challenging – because both sides involve convincing moral arguments.
- ◪ It opens the way for resolution.

In the current business environment, the compensation package for most senior executives buys one thing above all else: decision-making skills. This suggests two obvious points. First, businesses that make better decisions faster have an immense, bottom-line advantage over those that do not. Second, businesses have no room for managers who cannot or will not be decisive. Hard though it is to make the final choice – and tempting though it is to remain immersed in the engaging, challenging and clearly important realm of analysis – there comes a point when the decision must be made. Central to this is a clear, coherent process for resolving tough dilemmas.

Although many ethics programmes in corporations, schools, universities and professional groups spend a significant amount of time exploring case studies, they frequently provide only a minimal structure for doing so. Most notable for its absence is any methodology for arriving at a firm decision. Too often the discussion centres on two questions – "What would you do?" and "Why would you do it?" – without recourse to a clear framework that helps answer the second question. Too often, the long and noble traditions of moral philosophy are used to shed a pale academic light on the issue rather than to provide a vigorous, practical structure for decision-making.

In fact, these traditions can provide robust, flexible, potent principles for resolution. Three principles are especially helpful to those who need to make decisions. Each has behind it a legacy of philosophical thought and application. Each resonates with the intuitions of great numbers of people, reflecting standards they use to make decisions even if they have never thought about the philosophic tradition within which they are operating. Each is clearly under-standable in today's world. Each is practical, applicable and relevant. And each is remarkably different from the others. They are ends-based, rule-based, and care-based.[13]

Ends-based principle

Known in philosophical circles as Utilitarianism, this proposes that the most ethical decision is made when you do whatever produces the greatest good for the greatest number. Since you cannot be sure, ahead of time, what that good will be, or even, at times, where the greatest number will lie, you need to speculate as best you can on the consequences, or end, of your action.

The "ends-based" label is a reminder that, for the Utilitarian, it is appropriate to contemplate consequences in determining ethics. In fact, consequences are vital. Under this principle, if the consequences prove to be good, you did the right thing. If the consequences turn out badly, you did the wrong thing. If Alistair concludes that it is right not to report the Bosnia issue to the board because millions of people benefited despite modest levels of bribery, he is applying the ends-based principle.

Rule-based principle

The rule-based thinker holds to a principle formulated by Immanuel Kant known as the "categorical imperative". As Kant said: "I ought never to act except in such a way that I can also will that my maxim should become a universal law." Brought down to earth, Kant's principle requires that each person only performs those acts – or, more precisely, follows the "maxim" or rule – that they would like to see universalised. Put simply, it calls upon a person to ask: "Am I about to do something that I would like to see everyone in the entire world do in these circumstances?"

For Kant consequences were unimportant, in that the ethics of an act could never be determined simply by discovering how it turned out. Instead, what matters are the motives behind the act, and the rule that a person seeks to make universal.

If Sarah decided to warn Alan of his likely redundancy, she would apply the rule-based principle. The maxim that she most wants to follow is: "Always tell the truth, no matter what consequences follow."

Care-based principle

For some people, the ends-based principle seems invasive, like a busy-body who knows what is right and will determine it for you, and the rule-based principle seems stark and cold, not paying attention to real-life demands. These people are often drawn to the third, care-based principle of the "Golden Rule" that is central to all the world's great religions and says in its simplest form: "Do to others only what you would like them to do to you." As a principle of reversibility, it asks you to put yourself in someone else's shoes and ask how you would feel if you were treated in a particular way.

If Nigel imagined how it would feel to be John and face the threat of exclusion by his fellow workers, he might conclude that he would want the boss to intervene and help him find a way to keep his job. If he thinks that way, he is engaging the care-based principle.

Weighing the three principles

Going back to Janet's dilemma as a trustee of the non-profit organisation, it is easy see how each principle applies. If she adopts the ends-based principle and tries to do the greatest good for the greatest number, she will probably be led to think about consequences. She may well conclude that the outcome of punishing Ben, although important, takes a back seat to the more important outcome of the spin-off succeeding. Assessing probable futures, she may conclude that the risk of a major blow-up in the long term is less than the difficulty of negotiations with investors in the short term. In this way of thinking, the "greatest good" may be to keep the issue quiet.

But if Janet thinks like a Kantian and applies the rule-based principle, she may vote to expose Ben. She will reason that truth telling, however painful, is always the best course of action. She may conclude that you can never know the consequences of your actions with any certainty, and that the law of unintended consequences is apt to upset things in any case. She may also want to imagine that every trustee from every non-profit organisation in the world is watching, and that she is setting a standard that will endure forever. Does she want everyone to tell the truth always, or to do something else?

What if she thinks about the Golden Rule? As a care-based thinker, she will probably begin by asking: "If I were Ben, what would I want?" Her sense of compassion may override everything else, and she may decide to keep the matter quiet and give Ben a chance to redeem himself. But she may also see that there are other "others" in this "do to others" construct. What if she was an investor? What if she was the executive director of another non-profit organisation where Ben applies for a position? Conversely, what if she was one of Ben's children? Depending on where she sets her sights, she can reason through the care-based scenario in different ways.

This raises a vital point. These principles, along with the dilemma paradigms, do not provide a little black box that magically resolves dilemmas. Instead, they provide tools to help address tough choices.

Individuals still have to do the hard part – the thinking. But with these conceptual frameworks in place, they are more apt to make sound, thoughtful decisions, and more apt to be able to explain to others (and to themselves) why they chose as they did.

In Janet's case, she has ample reason to decide in either direction. Her choice will depend on the principle that, in this circumstance, she feels to be most persuasive. This should remind her of something else: her fellow trustees who make a different choice are not "wrong". They, too, come to principled and reasoned resolutions and are "right". This is not surprising. The dilemma paradigms had already explained that both sides of this dilemma were "right".

While this brief exposition of the three principles overlooks some of the nuances within them, it suggests several important things.

- There are at least three distinct ways of looking at the world through the lens of ethics. Each is noble, producing sound ethical decisions when applied carefully and thoughtfully to a tough dilemma.
- These three principles help explain why people of good will and sound character can arrive at radically different decisions about the same set of facts – decisions they feel are highly ethical, yet appear to be the polar opposite of the resolutions others select.
- Individuals seem to have no firm attachment to any one of these principles to the exclusion of the other two. It is not true, for example, that "once a Utilitarian, always a Utilitarian".

The IGE's research suggests that when participants in surveys are presented with a series of right-versus-right dilemmas and asked to explain the reasoning that led them to resolve each one as they did, they move in a fluid manner among the principles.[14] Applying different principles to different cases as seems most fitting, they appear to be searching for something other than consistency. Instead, they are seeking the best logic to explain the answer that, intuitively, they feel to be most satisfying.

In the end, this tells us something central about ethics. It is not a matter of conformity to a set of abstract, elaborate rules and practices. Instead, it is about the intuitions good people have as they try to find the best answer to the question of what they ought to do. The word "ought" is the centrepiece in the language of ethics. History is all about what was. Journalism is about what is. Futurism is about what will be. Law is about what must be. Ethics is about what ought to be.

The need for our global future, particularly in business, where decisions are increasingly complex, is for a language that allows us to address the tough right-versus-right decisions with the same clear, calm authority through which a historian describes what was or the journalist what is. Only in this way will a real decision-making capacity – a true "ethical fitness" – evolve.

5 The role of leadership

Mark Goyder and Peter Desmond

RADICAL CHANGES REQUIRE ADEQUATE AUTHORITY. A MAN MUST HAVE
INNER STRENGTH AS WELL AS INFLUENTIAL POSITION. WHAT HE DOES
MUST CORRESPOND WITH A HIGHER TRUTH.

Confucius

TODAY'S BUSINESS LEADERS can find themselves squeezed by a pincer of pressures. On one side is the pressure to show entrepreneurial flair by exploiting the commercial opportunities offered by new technology, globalisation and the new knowledge economy. On the other side, leaders need to respond to growing expectations and demands among customers and non-governmental organisations (NGOs) for greater accountability and social responsibility.

All businesses have an implicit "licence" to operate, whereby a number of stakeholders have given their tacit permission for the company to operate. As Figure 5.1 reveals, this licence requires leaders and their companies to satisfy a host of different requirements and expectations. Executive boards must earn the trust of their shareholders and demonstrate a consistent ability to deliver financial results. They must do so within an ethical framework that guarantees the sustainability of the enterprise and its social and ethical acceptability. A CEO attempting to develop separate and unlinked agendas for these two pressures risks corporate schizophrenia.

Leadership and values

Effective leadership is about striking a balance between hard-nosed entrepreneurial skills and corporate citizenship. It also entails translating the personal energy of an outstanding, entrepreneurial leader into the corporate energy of an enduring company. Ethics and values have a pivotal role in this process.

Enduring leadership – leadership that outlasts and transcends the individual – has been shown by research to be a predictor of long-term success. So investors who want a return over decades, and not just the short term, should pay attention to the long-term, enduring leadership culture of a business rather than the outstanding abilities of its current

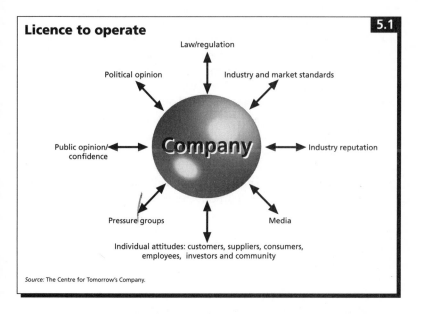

Licence to operate `5.1`

Law/regulation

Political opinion

Industry and market standards

Public opinion/confidence

Company

Industry reputation

Pressure groups

Media

Individual attitudes: customers, suppliers, consumers, employees, investors and community

Source: The Centre for Tomorrow's Company.

leader. Enduringly successful businesses display a strong DNA of purpose. They produce leaders who are "clock builders", not time-tellers.

The terms come from *Built to last*, a study of leadership and long-term shareholder value by James Collins and Jerry Porras of Stanford University.[1] They asked a cross-section of American business leaders to identify which companies, not individuals, they admired for visionary leadership. After eliminating companies founded after 1950, the portfolio of companies they were left with was found to have outperformed the stockmarket average over 50 years. The main difference between the visionary companies and the control group with which they were compared was in their approach to values. All the visionary companies had a powerful sense of their identity and what they wanted to achieve.

These findings were reinforced by the findings of the RSA Inquiry, *Tomorrow's Company*, which was published in 1995.[2] This was the result of three years' work by a group of UK business leaders who were challenged to come up with their vision of the successful company of the future. This report has been widely influential, leading to the foundation of the Centre for Tomorrow's Company. The reasoning can be summarised in the following propositions.

◪ Business is subordinate to society (it has a licence to operate).

- Every business is different (uniqueness).
- Businesses are started by individuals (entrepreneurs).
- Motives vary: profit or dividend for entrepreneur or shareholder is a necessary but rarely a sufficient motivation (the fallacy of *Homo Economicus*).
- The creation of sustainable shareholder value depends more than ever on inspiring loyalty, creativity, trust, mutual learning and feedback in all key relationships (business is about leadership through relationships).
- Companies cannot inspire these responses without generating a clear, pervasive, and enduring sense of the purpose and values of the whole organisation (purpose and values are the basis of leadership).

From these premises the Inquiry went on to make the case for an inclusive approach.

- Each business makes its own choices, but when it fails to include all key relationships in its definition and measurement of success (its success model) it misses opportunities, incurs undue risk and puts itself at a competitive disadvantage.
- Alongside business skills and strategy, purpose and values are central to the creation of shareholder value.
- Freedom of action – for both the individual and the business community – depends on the level of public confidence gained (licence to operate).

People and relationships

An inclusive approach starts as a leadership philosophy. It puts people and relationships at the heart of business success. There is no rigid formula: one of its key propositions is that every business is different.

An inclusive approach offers leaders a language of business success that makes equal sense to shareholders and to society. The most difficult task for shareholders is to judge the likelihood of an organisation delivering financial returns in the future. When Marks & Spencer, a British retailer, lost its way in the late 1990s, investors reacted only when the failings became apparent in reduced profits. Yet after the event insiders admitted that the clues were there in the changing reactions of customers and the company's reluctance to measure employee attitudes.

The challenge for any stakeholder is to get behind the rhetoric and

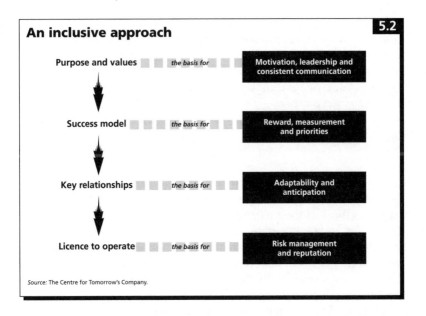

An inclusive approach 5.2

Purpose and values — *the basis for* → Motivation, leadership and consistent communication

↓

Success model — *the basis for* → Reward, measurement and priorities

↓

Key relationships — *the basis for* → Adaptability and anticipation

↓

Licence to operate — *the basis for* → Risk management and reputation

Source: The Centre for Tomorrow's Company.

find out what the company is really like – its attitude to and how it treats its employees and its suppliers, what its true values are, and its impact on communities and the environment.

An inclusive approach gives leaders and managers a framework, enabling them to work together on the things that they have said are important to them. It emphasises clarity of purpose and values, systems and mechanisms for performance measurement, reporting and dialogue. Most importantly, it stimulates leaders to extend performance measurement beyond the purely financial into other areas that affect its wellbeing and reputation in both the short and long term.

The Co-operative Bank in the UK is one company that has benefited greatly from adopting an inclusive approach. Ten years ago, the bank clearly defined the seven relationships on which it depends and began measuring the impact it has on each of them. Its annual *Partnership Report* contains information about the value the bank has created for its shareholders, customers, staff, suppliers and other stakeholders.

The Co-operative Bank aims to deliver value to all its partners in a balanced fashion over time, where "value" is defined by the partner, not the bank.[3]

77

> *In 2000, the bank produced a pre-tax profit of £96.3m, an increase of 9% compared with 1999 ... and the after tax return on equity was 22%. The outstanding commitment of staff is, in my view, probably the single most important reason for this success. In every staff survey conducted, we find quite extraordinary levels of pride in the bank as a leading promoter of ethical business practice.*
>
> Mervyn Pedelty, CEO, Co-operative Bank[4]

The bank measures its social responsibility and ecological impact. It publishes the results of surveys showing what its customers, staff and suppliers think of their relationship with the bank. It publicly sets itself targets for improvement in each relationship and reports openly on success or failure to meet these targets. For example, it asks suppliers how satisfied they are with their relationship with the bank. It also asks them about how the bank treats them compared with other companies, and whether they believe the bank acts with integrity.

There are five essential stages in an inclusive approach.

1 Purpose and values

Leaders have two jobs. One is to stimulate and drive the organisation they lead so that it survives, prospers and achieves its goals. The other – which is where leaders can make their biggest long-term contribution to their organisations – is to create the climate, the culture and the conditions that enable people, now and in the future, to contribute effectively to that performance.

As the pace of change develops, the second, transformational form of leadership becomes more important. This is harder to make time for, and is where using the practical framework of an inclusive approach is particularly helpful.

Global organisations need to involve leaders from across the span of the business if they are to arrive at a statement of their overarching purpose and values. These values should draw on shared beliefs across cultures about people and the values that guide the way they interact.

Questions that unlock this process include the following.

- Why do we exist?
- What makes us unique?
- What do we stand for?

◪ What are the things that we will never change – even if it costs us at least in the short term?

For example, Merck, a global pharmaceuticals company, says in its *Internal Management Guide*: "We are in the business of preserving and improving human life. All of our actions must be measured by our success in achieving this goal."[5]

Once the global statement of purpose and values is clear, people operating within various regions, countries or strategic business units should take these broad purposes and principles and express them locally in ways that will command attention and engage people emotionally. Each unit may need to employ different formats for translating loose values into codes of practice (which should be backed up by clear rewards and sanctions). These codes should pass two tests: the universal and the contextual. They should reflect the company's universal values yet still be applicable in different cultures.

ACHIEVING UNIVERSALITY IN DIVERSITY

Creating a universal sense of values in a business that operates across different cultures is easier said than done. The first step is to ensure that decision-makers understand the diversity involved in their key relationships. In their book *The Seven Cultures of Capitalism*, Charles Hampden Turner and Fons Trompenaars vividly illustrate cultural differences, drawing on the evidence of surveys of managers around the world.[6]

These surveys establish the attitudes of different cultures to ethical dilemmas; for example, the dilemma of loyalty to the company compared with loyalty to a friend. Managers considered the scenario of finding a supervisor, with whom they were friendly, drunk during the night shift. Should they put health and safety first and report him, or should they put friendship first and administer their own personal rebuke?

Respondents from Anglo-Saxon cultures placed greater emphasis on the needs of the organisation. Those from Asian cultures stressed the obligations of friendship. This story is an illustration of the first of six dilemmas that the authors explore. In a later book, they explain the close connection between different ways of looking at the world:

We finally noticed that foreign cultures are not arbitrarily or randomly different from one another. They are instead

mirror images of one another's values, reversals of the order
and sequence of looking and learning.[7]

For example, American culture starts with the resourceful individual, whereas Chinese culture says "the rice-growing village comes first". The authors argue that the important skill is to grasp the interdependence and importance of both propositions. This kind of intelligence is vital for those working in a cross-cultural world. It is no coincidence that non-conformists constitute ten times, and Quakers 40 times, the proportion of entrepreneurs that would be suggested by their numbers, or that Indian and Chinese immigrants make up one-third of the engineering workforce of Silicon Valley's high-tech firms. Outsiders and minorities are often forced to reconcile opposites and invent new ways of earning a living in inhospitable surroundings.

An inclusive approach in a diverse world requires sensitivity to local traditions, and the acceptance that in different cultures it may be necessary to use different ways of making sure that a business keeps to its overarching principles in pursuit of its aims. And keep to them it should. For many years, international diversity was used as an excuse for ethical inaction, an attitude that helps perpetuate price-fixing, restrictive practices, bribery and corruption, and many other barriers to world-class performance. If corporate leaders do not stand firm on their corporate principles, why should those that they lead be minded to do so?

MAKING IT MEANINGFUL

The best companies arrive at a statement of purpose and values in an inclusive way and revisit it regularly. It is not enough to settle for the ideas hit upon by senior executives during a weekend in a country hotel. The net must be stretched much wider to include managers and others in all locations.

It is the sense of ownership of the words and principles that doubles the likelihood of their implementation. Mechanisms are needed to maintain a sense of ownership. In the John Lewis Partnership, a leading British retailer, the founder embodied the purpose and values of the company in its constitution. An elected governance structure was also created within each store and across the company as a whole that continually holds the management to account for its performance against this purpose.

In some companies, values are preached but not practised. If a company's stated values include teamwork, but people are rewarded entirely for individual performance, the stated value soon becomes hollow. Leaders who frequently visit different sites and listen to their people make a more powerful statement about the company's values than does anything that is written down.

2 Identify and review key relationships

Anything a company achieves is through its relationships. In the age of the Internet, this is becoming true in a different way. For example, the Internet reduces more and more products to commodities. A company's managers need to think through which of its relationships are transactional – merely price-driven – and which will benefit from the building of intimacy and trust.

A review of key relationships may also reveal opportunities to turn transactions into relationships, perhaps by making the brand more distinctive and thereby helping people feel differently about the product and company. A set of strong underlying values can prove valuable anchors in this process. For example, Sainsbury's, a leading British retailer, has been exploring the idea of the "experience economy" and has decided to base its strategy on the idea of retailing as entertainment. However, it has said that it will do so in a way that is consistent with its reputation for affordable, quality food.

CHALK AND CHEESE CAN BE INCLUSIVE

One of the UK's most successful retail developments came from the bold decision by Lend Lease Europe to take a derelict chalk pit at Bluewater in Kent and convert it into a major shopping centre for south-east England. It has been a winner in terms of sales, quality of building and ambience, community engagement and every other measure. Lend Lease's shares have delivered compound annual growth of 24% over 40 years.

Lend Lease has turned transcending limits – limits defined by industry, geography, or capability – into a core competence. "We want to create things that are extraordinary, feasible, and valuable," says Ann McCallum of Lend Lease Corporate Solutions. "Everything we do has to fit all three criteria."[8]

Lend Lease developed its "Ten Commandments" – the priorities that would define Bluewater. It took great care in the selection of its partners and in ensuring their commitment to this vision. Much of the project's success is owed to the company's inclusive approach to all partners, including the local community. Lend Lease cultivated these relationships not only through joint tasks, but also through social and community activities. This helped to reinforce a sense of teamwork and human contact between partners.

One set of innovations involved the construction process. The Bluewater team hired 400 construction workers off the long-term unemployment rolls. In partnership with local training agencies, the team also created the Bluewater Foundation, which provided skills to 8,200 construction workers.

Bluewater not only digitised the construction site by installing an intranet for automating the contract-approval process, it also humanised the construction area. Workers were asked what benefits they would most like to have on-site – a question they had never been asked before – and ended up with benefits ranging from an on-site chaplain to state-of-the-art showers to a diverse set of catering options. The surrounding community, meanwhile, benefited from the creation of the Bluewater Pages, a directory of prequalified local businesses (including everything from accounting firms to window cleaners) – which made it easy for the more than 40 contractors working on-site to employ locals.

A year away from the project's due date, the Foundation shifted its focus from developing construction skills to providing comprehensive, ongoing education for those who would hold the 7,000 permanent retail jobs created by the centre. The idea ... was not just to train retail workers for casual jobs but also in the crucial design and construction partnership between Lend Lease and to help them jump-start their careers.[9]

In the construction partnership with Bovis, for example, leaders on both sides resisted pressure from their subordinates to put up the usual signs advertising the individual companies in the development. There were only Bluewater signs, such was the determination of both leaders to suppress territorial jealousy and promote commitment to the project and its ultimate customers.

Bluewater's scale was matched only by the speed of its completion. Lend Lease's 250-person development team, along with 40 contractors, countless subcontractors, and more than 20,000 construction workers, guided the project from initial conception to the final leasing stage in just 1,628 days. The project came in two weeks ahead of schedule, on budget, and fully leased. Since the grand opening of Bluewater, in March of this year [1999], an average of more than 75,000 people per day have visited the complex.[10]

THE ETHICAL DIMENSION

As leaders work through their key relationships, they should start thinking about the ethical dimension. They may be utterly dependent upon suppliers. How will they choose those suppliers? If their suppliers do not have the same views on disclosure and transparency, they could put the company in a dishonest position with its customers. How should a supplier's ethics be screened? When pressurising suppliers on cost and price, how can the company ensure that they do not cut corners which compromise safety, service or other value components?

The review of key relationships also ensures that issues of cultural diversity are faced. Complex organisations have relationships that cut across boundaries of international culture and also across the boundaries of professional discipline, experience, religious observance, approaches to gender and so on. A good review of key relationships will bring these differences out and make it easier for people to work together across these boundaries.

The same process should be applied during the due diligence phase of an acquisition, a critical change in a company's key relationships. Cisco Systems, a giant high-tech company, has acquired over 40 companies. It insists on a due diligence process that extends over the purpose, values, culture and ethics of the target company. Even if there is a fit in the strategy, the technology and the products, CEO John Chambers refuses to make an acquisition if the target company does not share Cisco's perceptions and values:

> This is an empowerment culture, a customer focused culture, a culture of equals. If someone has an office four times the size of mine, if all the stock options are at the top of the

organisation and there is no mention of customers, we don't touch that company.[11]

3 Define success

A success model defines what a business does uniquely well and creates the framework for measurement. This means looking at the leading indicators, such as employee retention rates and customer satisfaction, that help predict future success, as well as the lagging indicators, such as revenues, that derive from actions taken in the past.

Think about the ethical dimension of success. If you define success simply in terms of financial results, with no description of the ethical context, do not be surprised when people cheat to achieve them. If you intend your company to be around in ten years time, it is vital that you set down some guidance to ensure that your reputation is upheld.

Ethics and performance: an example from IBM
As early as 1961 I circulated a standard of ethics about what our people could and could not do. There were rules against bare-knuckle selling practices, such as disparaging other companies' products or leaking information about machines we hadn't yet announced in order to block a competitor from making a sale. Perhaps most important, I told the salesmen that in fighting for orders they had to show a sense of fair play.
Tom Watson Junior, president of IBM

Mr Watson's 1961 note to salesmen included these words:
Turn the situation around. Suppose that you were a competitor – small, precariously financed, without a large support organisation, and without a big reputation in the field, but with a good product. How would you feel if the big IBM company took the action which you propose to take?[12]

4 Measure and reward performance

At General Electric, CEO Jack Welch simplified performance measurement into three categories: cash, employee satisfaction and customer satisfaction. Many businesses have now adopted their own form of balanced scorecard, because "what gets measured gets managed". It is vital that a measurement framework gives the board a total view of the business. Such a framework helps send a consistent message to employees that ethics matter. The Co-operative Bank has ensured that in all its stakeholder relationships, managers are required to use at least one measure of success that is related to ethical behaviour.

5 *Communicate with all stakeholders: dialogue that leads to change*
The true potential of a company to create wealth is the combined creative potential of its leadership and its relationships. Long-term success depends on sharing and shaping an understanding of a company's purpose, values and aims through dialogue with stakeholders. Dialogue is by definition a two-way process, a chance for the company to set out its stall and for others to communicate their ideas and expectations. It should not be a token gesture but a process that feeds the innovation of a company. When the CEO of a big international company, who had been waxing lyrical about stakeholder dialogue, was asked by one of the authors of this chapter to quote an example of what changes have been implemented as a result of stakeholder dialogue, he could not think of one.

Dialogue implies openness of mind. This cuts both ways. Companies may need to view their operations against a wider set of social ethics than previously. Equally, stakeholder groups need to understand the values espoused by the company. Just as some companies have no intention of changing direction through dialogue, some stakeholder groups have made up their minds about a company without even attempting to enquire about its values and purpose. The activists targeting Huntingdon Life Sciences are not going to change their position because of stakeholder dialogue. There is more point in dialogue with groups whose values allow for a changing of their stance in the light of the evidence.

Nestlé, the largest food company in the world, with an annual turnover of around $50 billion, has clearly thought hard about its own purpose and values, yet it is still regarded by many as "unethical" because of its stance on baby nutrition and genetically modified foods. There is never likely to be agreement about difficult ethical issues. The key to managing ethically based risk and opportunity is to ensure that ethical debates and arguments occur within the parameters of a company's values. In this way the company need not be defensive. Stakeholder groups also benefit because if they understand the company's ethical framework, they are more likely to construct arguments that have a chance of being considered in the boardroom.

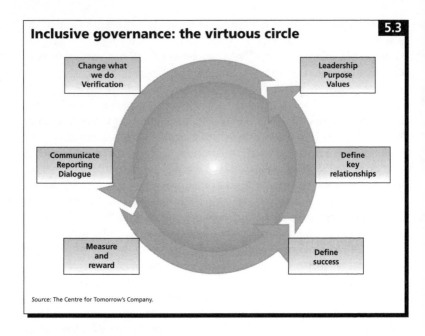

Inclusive governance: the virtuous circle

5.3

- Change what we do Verification
- Leadership Purpose Values
- Communicate Reporting Dialogue
- Define key relationships
- Measure and reward
- Define success

Source: The Centre for Tomorrow's Company.

The Nestlé approach

Values

A clear set of values was drawn together by Peter Brabeck, when he became CEO. These values were publicised widely – to all stakeholders and anyone with an interest, including the competition. They are the bedrock for all operations, anywhere in the world.

Method

Nestlé believes that long-term sustainable improvement depends on people, not financial instruments. The business is decentralised to meet local needs and tastes and to build local presence and trust. However, operational activities such as logistics and supply-chain management operate centrally to get the benefit of volume and co-ordinated management.

Leadership

Mr Brabeck believes in involvement, engagement and action. He visits all plants, speaks to lots of people, engages them, listens to them, challenges them and acts. He encourages aggression, courage and self-motivation and is always looking out for new leaders.

The bottom line
The effect of having clear values and participative leadership is a reinvigorated company showing steady growth in both turnover and profit; with a capitalisation that grew from SFr55 billion in 1997 to SFr150 billion in 2000.

Decision-making
Nestlé works hard to be objective. For example, on the issue of genetically modified foods, Mr Brabeck was quoted in the Harvard Business Review as saying: "We asked eminent professors to write their opinions about genetic technology for us – positive or negative. We reviewed what the professors had to say, discussed it, and concluded that genetic engineering is a technology that is good for humankind." To try to allay fears, Nestlé has a well-publicised written commitment to responsible marketing.

As others see things
Criticism
However, different interpretations come to the fore with infant formula milk. The press and some international observers claim that Nestlé has been breaking the law for over 26 years by not labelling containers in the right language and by failing to take account of the poor state of a country's water. It is accused of contributing to the spread of disease among infants by promoting bottle-feeding to the detriment of breastfeeding.

The dilemma
Ethical choices
Nestlé's dilemma is between what it sees as scientific and economic logic, and the perceived impact on parts of the world community. Even if it were to be convinced that the impact of formula milk was negative, it would have to consider the needs of the shareholders in the phasing in of any withdrawal of such a strategic product given its significant financial implications.[13]

Inclusive approach to ethics: costs and benefits
Many companies have seen shareholder value destroyed as a result of

ethical issues and their implementation – for example Barings, Perrier, Texaco and Tomkins. But there is plenty of evidence that an ethical, inclusive approach is good for business. It is instructive to contrast Shell, which was one of the first companies to have and apply a statement of business principles, with a much younger company, Intel, whose story is told by Tim Jackson.[14] The early days of the company, in the late 1960s, were characterised by a spirit of adventure. Gordon Moore and Bob Noyce, the two founders, would interview young engineers across plastic tables at a pancake house. They had to be willing to take a pay cut and a demotion; if they came, it would be because of their faith in the brilliance and ambition of the founders and the career growth, stock options and exciting work that would follow. The organisation was also determinedly non-hierarchical: it believed in "knowledge power" not "position power".

Twenty-five years later, with sales of $6 billion, the ethos had changed. The company had become arrogant and aggressive towards its competitors, and employees who left to set up their own businesses were threatened with legal action.

Perhaps the formative moment in the evolution of Intel from the adventurous and attractive start-up to the political, inward-focused and arrogant culture came in 1971 when Intel's fourth man, Bob Graham, departed. Noyce and Moore hired Graham as head of sales. He joined shortly after Andy Grove, who was to be head of operations and eventually became the company's president.

> The last straw for Graham was a dispute over something
> apparently trivial: the data sheets ... that Intel sent to
> engineers, providing technical specifications and
> performance information.[15]

Bob Graham discovered that the bipolar drivers designed to work with the new 1103 memory chip would not work across the chip's full temperature range. Andy Grove rejected any solution to the temperature problem as too costly. Although it was unlikely to bother many customers, Graham insisted that Intel make the problem clear on the data sheets.

Grove and Graham argued more and more bitterly. Eventually Noyce was called in to adjudicate. Graham was told to issue the data sheets without making the problem known. Grove had won.

*On his way from the confrontation to his lunch date with
his wife, Mr Graham cleared his desk. He wasn't fired; he
had simply been presented with an ultimatum: either leave
or publish the data sheet the way Mr Grove wanted. At that
moment he recalled that it was precisely to get away from
issues of politics and style that he had left his former
company and joined Intel. If Intel was going to revert to the
characteristics of his old employer, he wanted no further
part in the venture.*

*[Mr Graham's departure] marked a turning point in the
structure of Intel's leadership ... It would be another 15 years
before Grove received the title of chief executive, but from
1971 onwards, he was to be the dominant influence over the
company and its culture.*[16]

Intel's moment of truth arrived in the autumn of 1994. There was an
error in the Pentium chip. The circumstances in which the error would
affect users were rare: for the average Pentium owner only once in 27,000
years. But for rocket designers, or mathematicians running complex
calculations continuously, the frequency could be as much as once a day.

Intel faced an ethical decision with powerful implications for its
reputation. The cost of declaring the bug would be potentially tens of
millions of dollars. The defect could be replaced in the next series of
upgrades. Intel took the same kind of decision that Andy Grove had
fought for when Bob Graham was ousted: it decided to keep the bug
secret.[17]

It was a mathematician who discovered the bug. He received a casual
brush-off from the technical support line, which told him that the
problem must be somewhere else in his system. By this time the company
had known about the bug for five months. A month later a new Usenet
group was set up on the Internet called alt.jokes.Pentium. Jokes appearing
on the site included:

Q: What does Pentium stand for?
*A: Perfect Enough for Nine out of Ten Instructors at the
University of Montana.*
Or: Practically Everyone Now Thinks Its Useless for Maths.

A few days later, CNN, an American cable news network, was on the
case. Intel's stock price had fallen 72%. IBM stopped shipment of all

Pentium parts. At an emergency meeting, the Intel board reversed its previous decision. The cost was $475m.[18]

Shell and Intel will never be the same, but it is interesting to contrast the likely fortunes of the two companies. One has a clear set of principles by which to guide its actions. The other appears to have no clear code of ethics and to operate according to utilitarian principles, such as: "What can we get away with?" Whereas Shell appears to have moved beyond individual leaders setting the ethical tone, the evidence from Tim Jackson's book is that Intel appears far more dependent on the influence of strong controlling individuals.

Effective leadership is about laying the foundations for the efficient and the ethical conduct of business. An integrated view of ethics and economics is logical and inevitable. What is deeply illogical is the separation of value and values, reason and feeling. The inclusive approach offers leaders a practical way of pursuing economic goals in a way that is calculated to inspire confidence, loyalty and ethical probity. It is a necessity, not a luxury, for the successful organisation of tomorrow.

6 Corporate governance: the stakeholder debate

Daniel Summerfield

THE MAIN PURPOSE OF THE BOARD OF DIRECTORS IS TO SEEK TO ENSURE
THE PROSPERITY OF THE COMPANY BY COLLECTIVELY DIRECTING THE
COMPANY'S AFFAIRS, WHILST MEETING THE APPROPRIATE INTERESTS OF ITS
SHAREHOLDERS AND RELEVANT STAKEHOLDERS.
Institute of Directors, Standards for the Board, 1999

IN RECENT YEARS there has been growing interest in the ethical issues
faced by boards of directors as they attempt to balance the competing
demands of those concerned with the success of a company. Chapter 5
explored the concepts of inclusive leadership and corporate accountability, which have given impetus to the debate about the nature of
stakeholders' rights and how they stand compared with those of
shareholders.

Underlying this debate is a change in the way business success is
assessed and achieved. Current bottom-line profits are increasingly seen
as just one, albeit critical, success factor. Studies on both sides of the
Atlantic have shown the weight now being attached to the concept of
corporate social responsibility (CSR), which takes in such factors as being
a good employer, protecting the environment and being socially
responsible. The results of a 1998 survey of the world's most respected
companies, as reported in the *Financial Times*, showed that when asked
to rank the attributes that would make a company most respected in the
future, chief executives placed "robust and human corporate culture" just
below "strong and consistent profit performance". Furthermore, a 1998
Institute of Directors' report, *Sign of the Times*, identified honesty and
integrity as the most important additional personal qualities required by
new appointments to the board. Commitment and loyalty were ranked
second. All this has profound implications for corporate governance.

Director's duties: a legal patchwork

In the UK corporate governance model, with its unitary board structure,
directors owe their fiduciary duties to the company. This means that they

are required to act in good faith in the best interests of the company, exercise their powers for the proper purposes for which they were conferred and not place themselves in a position where there is conflict (actual or potential) between their duties to the company and their personal interests or duties to third parties. Their duties are owed to the company, not the shareholders or stakeholders – though they are accountable to the shareholders for the stewardship of the company. The statutory duties of directors towards other parties beside the company are minimal. Indeed there is no explicit duty (in a solvent company) to stakeholders such as employees, customers, suppliers and the wider community.

In Continental Europe, the situation is somewhat different. In Germany, for example, which has a two-tier board structure – a supervisory board and a management board – the duty of directors to the company is more widely expressed than in Britain to include employees and the public interest. In France, split boards with employee participation have been introduced as an optional alternative to the traditional single board.

Changing times

Is the law out of step with the realities of today's business world of complex interdependent relationships? Some will take the view that it is. Others will argue that it is a matter of how the law is interpreted. What is undeniable is that the business world continues to evolve, and, therefore, directors must adapt to its changes and take them into account in their decision-making.

The law may stop short of granting rights to stakeholders, but, in reality, many directors consider their interests because failing to do so would probably damage the interests of the company. Directors must now be concerned with the multiple effects their company has on society, from the way it treats its employees, suppliers and customers, to such issues as the environment, child labour and health and safety. And for global companies that concern must extend to the many different cultures in which they operate.

For example, BP's governance policy, which among other things embraces ethical conduct, employee relationships, and health, safety and environmental (HSE) performance, states that the CEO "will not cause or permit anything to be done without taking into account the effect on long-term shareholder value of the health, safety and environmental consequences of the action, and the political consequences".[1] Conversely, the widespread initial view that corporate social responsibility might confuse existing business objectives has given way to a growing realisation that the implementation of a sound policy can provide real benefits for the shareholder – making it an important issue for the board. Arguably, one of the most difficult tasks for directors is to weigh up the short- and long-term interests of the company and then decide on the right course of action to take.

In some situations, the longer term benefits to the company of making a decision that is prompted by the interests of other stakeholders may be difficult to quantify: indeed there may be immediately identifiable short-term disadvantages to the company. In these circumstances, directors may be concerned that, in the absence of any specific duty outside company law to act in a specific way, acting in the interests of stakeholders could give rise to a legal challenge that they had breached their fiduciary duties to the company.

However a board decides to treat its stakeholders (which will change as circumstances change), the important point is that it recognises it has to take a view and maintains what it regards as a proper balance of interests. It is the board's responsibility to lay down principles to follow in relation to stakeholders and to monitor the way those principles are put into effect.

The role of independent directors

The broad perspective and independent judgment of non-executive directors can be immensely helpful in determining a company's approach towards ethical issues and stakeholder interests. In addition to challenging existing practices, they should be in a position to contribute knowledge and experience of good practice. They should play a central role in setting CSR policy and in ensuring that sufficient rigour is being applied to business processes supporting CSR activities.

For these reasons, some companies, such as Shell and Rio Tinto, have CSR committees that are composed entirely of non-executive directors. An alternative approach is to give a particular independent director specific responsibility for monitoring CSR-related issues, both internally and externally.

CSR issues can be wide ranging and unique to the company in question, so the challenge for non-executive directors is to select the key questions that provide the greatest opportunity for disclosing internal practices. Some suggestions for these questions[2] include:

- Is there accountability for managing CSR issues within a company's governance framework?
- Do supporting performance reporting processes exist at both a corporate and regional level?
- Does a formal mechanism exist for capturing stakeholder concerns and for providing them with feedback on progress?
- How are company expectations of CSR behaviours communicated to suppliers and business partners?
- How does a company gain assurance that regional behaviours are aligned with corporate values?

Parity for stakeholders?

According to a recent report from the Ashridge Centre for Business and Society, over one-third of *Fortune* 500 companies have decided not to proceed with proposed investment projects because of ethical or environmental concerns.[3]

A similar trend is apparent in the UK. *Ethics in Business*, a survey by the UK's Institute of Directors (IOD) in 1999 of 850 of its members, revealed that many boards of directors are giving greater priority to broader stakeholder interests. The survey shows that respondents have mixed views about the statement: "We see shareholders' interests as our first priority". Although 42% agreed with the statement to some degree, 27% completely disagreed. As Figure 6.1 shows, there was neither clear agreement nor disagreement about the primary importance of profits and shareholders. Ten years ago a stronger endorsement of these two factors might have been expected. The survey also reveals that boards are now trying to strike a balance between the interests of shareholders and those of other stakeholders.

Shareholder activism

Another issue that should be considered by directors is the role of shareholders, particularly institutional investors, and their expectations of and influence over the company's attitude towards CSR. On both sides of the Atlantic, many companies are facing increasing pressure from activists who are using shareholder resolutions and proxy solicitation to influence company policy on social and environmental issues.

The development and growth of what is now known as socially responsible investing (SRI) has according to Garry Topp, SRI fund manager at Henderson Global Investors, gone through three stages.

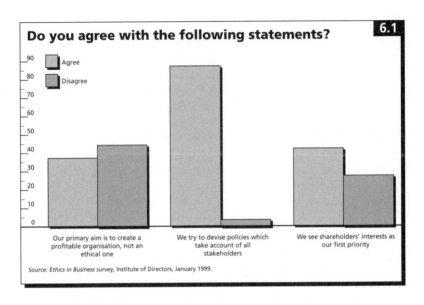

Do you agree with the following statements? `6.1`

Legend:
- Agree
- Disagree

Categories:
- Our primary aim is to create a profitable organisation, not an ethical one
- We try to devise policies which take account of all stakeholders
- We see shareholders' interests as our first priority

Source: *Ethics in Business survey*, Institute of Directors, January 1999.

At first the major concern of investors was to exclude companies in certain fields such as arms, tobacco, pornography or gambling. Later environmental factors were added – "green investing". The emphasis moved from negative to positive – from exclusions to inclusions. More recently the wider concept of responsibility in investing has developed. Sustainability is one such element – are the companies engaging in activities that will lead to sustainable activities, such as switching from fossil fuels to renewable fuels?[4]

Craig Mackenzie, ethical manager for Friends Ivory & Sime (which pioneered ethical investment on a large scale and now runs the UK's largest ethical unit trust) believes that this kind of watch on ethical and social issues is increasingly viewed by companies as part of "good corporate governance".[5]

sri is being driven not just from the bottom up by retail investors' demands, but top-down from governments. In July 2000, for example, a new UK law came into force requiring UK pension funds to disclose the extent (if any) to which "social, environmental or ethical concerns are taken into account in the selection, retention and realisation of investments". This means that pension fund trustees must disclose in their statement of investment principles what, if any, consideration is given to ethical issues. In turn, directors can expect more questions about their stakeholder relations and ethical performance.

The UK has led the way in Europe in this area, but other countries are catching up. France has adopted new regulations on ethical disclosure similar to the UK's and Germany is producing its own guidelines.

Corporate responsibility: different approaches

In the UK, a debate has been taking place about whether it should follow some US States in introducing so-called "stakeholder statutes" which could give directors a legal duty to take the interests of the broader community into consideration when making decisions.

The 1998 report from the UK Committee on Corporate Governance, chaired by Sir Ronald Hampel, concluded that:

> To redefine the directors' responsibilities in terms of the
> stakeholders would mean identifying all the various
> stakeholder groups; and deciding the nature and extent of
> the directors' responsibility to each. The result would be that
> the directors were not effectively accountable to anyone
> since there would be no clear yardstick for judging their
> performance. This is a recipe neither for good governance
> nor for corporate success.

Similarly, the central corporate governance issue of the current UK Company Law Review was whether to stick with the approach that companies should be run so as to maximise shareholder value or change to a pluralist model which would put greater emphasis on the needs of "stakeholders" alongside those of shareholders. The steering group initially outlined two different approaches.

Enlightened shareholder value

Supporters of this approach believe that no reform of the fundamentals of directors' duties is required because "the ultimate objective of companies as currently enshrined in law – ie to generate maximum value for shareholders – is in principle the best means ... of securing overall prosperity and welfare".[6]

Pluralist

Proponents of a pluralist approach argue that "the ultimate objective of maximising shareholder value will not achieve maximum prosperity and welfare". They believe that companies should be required to serve a wider range of interests, and that the interests of shareholders should not override those of the company's stakeholders.

The Company Law Review steering group is likely to propose to government that an "inclusive" approach be taken towards directors' duties. If adopted, this will require directors to have regard to all the relationships on which the company depends with a view to achieving company success for the collective benefit of shareholders. Legal accountability for the stewardship of the company will continue to be to shareholders, but the law would acknowledge that directors' decisions should take account of the long term and the wider community.

What do directors think?

The IOD's 1999 survey, *Company Law Review: The Stakeholder Debate* reveals that more than eight out of ten respondents firmly rejected the idea that there should be a legal requirement upon directors to take ethical and social considerations into account when making decisions. This suggests that a flexible approach is needed, one that allows directors to act in ways they think are appropriate in the circumstances rather than having to act according to rigid rules.

Every company is different and it is the directors who are most likely to appreciate the nature of the company's shareholder and stakeholder relationships, and who are therefore best placed to make the appropriate judgments on ethical standards and practices. Legislation that constrains them from doing that could undermine what has been achieved by voluntary actions in this area and may risk companies opting for boiler plate and box-ticking approaches that satisfy their legal obligations but which are, in practice, meaningless.

Training directors

As their responsibilities grow and become more complex, there is an increasing pressure on directors to develop their professional standards and to undergo training. This is particularly relevant for implementing ethical standards and practices and in understanding how to balance and deal with the potentially competing demands of shareholder and stakeholder groups.

The Chartered Director professional qualification – the world's first professional qualification for company directors – aims to promote a high standard of integrity and professionalism in the boardroom and builds upon many years of effort by the IOD to provide professional development opportunities for company directors, to set and promote good boardroom standards, and generally to foster a professional approach to the running of UK companies.

A code of conduct lays down the standards of professionalism and ethics expected of chartered directors. To help focus them on the importance of stakeholders, Article 4 of the code stipulates that chartered directors shall "exercise responsibilities to employees, customers, suppliers and other relevant stakeholders, including the wider community".

The code further advises that while the obligations of a director are primarily owed to the company, it is also necessary to take into account the interests of all individuals and groups that the board judges have a legitimate interest in the achievement of company objectives and the way in which they are achieved. A director should ensure that the board identifies and knows the interests, views and expectations of these stakeholders – and that communications with such parties are "timely, effective and unbiased, subject to the needs of commercial security and regulatory compliance where appropriate".

Chartered directors are expected to help their boards to promote goodwill with stakeholders and be prepared to be accountable for company actions. They are also advised to encourage their boards to set up procedures for managing relationships with stakeholders, particularly at times of crisis (eg litigation, environmental disasters, takeover bids).

Private profit and public good

> Now will come the era of corporate image, in which
> consumers will increasingly make purchases on the basis of
> a firm's whole role in society: how it treats employees,
> shareholders and local neighbourhoods.[7]

The evidence from the UK suggests that the best approach is to encourage rather than force businesses to take stakeholder interests into account. If CSR can be shown to be good for business then more directors will be in favour of it. In practice, however, the business case may rest more on the damage that unethical behaviour can do to a company's reputation and brand value, which the consultancy Interbrand has calculated may account for up to 25% of the world's financial wealth.[8]

But is there a link between good corporate citizenship and financial performance? In his report published in 1999 for the non-profit

Conference Board business group, David Vidal found that:

> Although bottom-line evidence of [good] citizenship's benefits
> is scarce, anecdotal validation in the form of enhanced
> corporate image, customer preference, strong employee
> relations and smoother regulatory approvals is proliferating
> in both the US and the UK.[9]

What research does exist, he adds, shows that good corporate citizenship is not harmful to shareholder value and in specific instances can be shown to have added to it. Speaking to the London Business School, Michael Porter, a professor at Harvard Business School, said

> in a more socially and environmentally aware world,
> corporate responsibility in these spheres will itself be a
> source of competitive advantage.[10]

Both old and new companies now make a point of highlighting their ethical principles. For example, Unilever, a multinational company, believes that:

> Economic growth must go hand in hand with sound
> environmental management, equal opportunities worldwide
> and the highest standards of health and safety in factories
> and offices.[11]

Such statements suggest that many businesses now acknowledge that they have a wider responsibility. By going on record to say this, they invite those in the wider world to judge a company's actions by its stated principles.

Positive lessons

It is clear that a one-size-fits-all approach to promoting ethical standards and CSR has little appeal for the current generation of business leaders. Each company needs to develop its own particular code, one that reflects its own particular circumstances, culture and environment. Simply importing a "standard" code will, in most cases, be counter-productive. Unilever supports this view stating that:

> A company will have to formulate its own standards and
> values to supplement the laws and regulations in the
> various countries. It will have to ensure that these are
> accepted internally and complied with.

Directors need to be convinced that adopting particular standards is
in their company's best interests. Putting it more bluntly, they need to be
convinced of the competitive advantage that might be gained from
raising their ethical standards both internally and externally.

The effects of good corporate citizenship are hard to measure beyond
the general findings of studies conducted on both sides of the Atlantic
that imply that it is beneficial to company financial performance. One
way in which directors may be convinced is through the example of
companies they admire, supported by research, that identifies best ethical
practices. After all, it is much easier to come to a decision if you know
that you are following in the tracks of people who have made the same
decision and profited from it.

This, together with professional training, will not only improve the
standards adopted generally by companies but also introduce the
necessary level of support from the boardroom to ensure effective
implementation – an area which, to date, is causing many companies
some difficulty.

7 Building a sustainable reputation

Oonagh Harpur

THE BENEFIT OF THE BENCHMARKING RESEARCH HAS BEEN TO ALLOW THE
ORGANISATION TO CARRY OUT AN AUDIT OF ITS CONSCIENCE AND OF ITS
PRACTICES, TO TAKE STOCK AND REFOCUS ON THOSE PARTS OF THE
BUSINESS, WHICH ARE OFTEN IGNORED. IT HELPED CREATE A NEW WAY OF
THINKING AND FROM A REALLY PRACTICAL PERSPECTIVE GAVE US SOME OF
THE MEANS TO MOVE THE BUSINESS IN A NEW DIRECTION.
Dan Wright, managing director, Catering & Allied

SINCE MICHAEL PORTER revolutionised business strategy with his work
on competitive advantage in the early 1980s, corporate reputation and
branding have been driven from the outside in. The challenge for chief
executives has been to analyse the market place, determine the best
market position and re-brand the business accordingly. Brands have been
largely driven by market demand: what customers desire, at prices they
will buy.

Today, however, companies are viewing their brands as a set of values
and beliefs, even a distinct corporate personality, that has the potential
to attract customers and inspire their commitment and loyalty. Business
success can hinge on the perception of a brand's attributes and appeal
compared with those of competing brands, thus highlighting the need for
brands to be nurtured, managed, sustained and protected.

Many companies now have a strong brand backed by mission, vision
and values statements. But there can be a large gap between what these
say and how a company conducts its operations. There have been a
number of well-publicised cases where companies have failed to align
their brands with their core purposes and values and have found their
reputation damaged by accusations of hypocrisy and exploitative or
unethical behaviour.

This chapter sets out how a company can build a sustainable
reputation. The "inside-out" approach it outlines is based on the
National Forum on the purpose and values of business led jointly by the
Institute of Directors (IOD) and the Royal Society for the Encouragement
of the Arts, Manufactures and Commerce (RSA) in 1998–1999.

The Forum established common purposes and values at the heart of all businesses in Britain. It also developed a method for measuring the extent to which a company's purpose and values are reflected in its operations as experienced by its customers, employees, suppliers, investors, directors and the wider community.

An "inside-out" job

Companies can try to minimise reputational risk by improving corporate governance, publishing codes of conduct, and by setting and auditing social, ethical and environmental standards. In many cases, the change process is also driven from the outside in. The question often asked is: "What values do our products need to communicate if we are to attract more customers?"

Building a sustainable reputation is primarily an inside-out process. Glossy PR and advertising may result in a short-term improvement in reputation, but it will not convince a sceptical press and increasingly sophisticated investors, customers and employees. A sustainable reputation can only be built from the inside, starting with what a company or organisation is, what its business is here to do and how it goes about it: its purposes and values. When a firm is clear about these it can look at redefining its brand to reflect them. Rather than becoming a "me too" company, the business gains a competitive advantage by defining its brand in a way that plays to its strengths and differentiates it from its competitors.

Several major studies have revealed the impact of clear purposes and values on business performance. For example, James Collins and Jerry Porras conducted a six-year study at Stanford University of visionary companies which was published in their book *Built to Last*. The researchers found that visionary companies like Hewlett-Packard, Procter & Gamble and Ford differentiate themselves by:

- stressing continuity of values;
- investing in people;
- having objectives in addition to a profit objective.

From 1926 to 1990, the shares of these and similar visionary companies outperformed the American market average by a factor of 16.

In the UK, the RSA led a national inquiry from 1993 to 1995 entitled *Tomorrow's Company*. The study concluded that tomorrow's successful company would be inclusive, building long-term positive relationships with customers, suppliers, employees, shareholders and the community.

It would have a clear statement of its purposes and values and would communicate these consistently.

Building a sustainable reputation

REPUTATION IS WHAT IS GENERALLY BELIEVED OR SAID ABOUT AN
INDIVIDUAL OR ORGANISATION.

Concise Oxford Dictionary

An organisation's reputation distinguishes it from its competitors and is its primary source of competitive advantage. Reputation takes years to build and can be lost overnight.

A company's reputation is built on what people believe or say about it. People form their beliefs from their personal experience of the company and what they read, hear or see about it. People typically first learn about a new product through advertising, word of mouth or the media, which helps to create a certain set of expectations. Customers who buy the product build on this as they judge whether it comes up to their expectations. A sustainable reputation is built on repeated transactions and experiences with the company, leading to a relationship between the customer and the company.

In theory, the process of building a sustainable reputation is simple. In practice, identifying the individuals and groups who can have an important impact on company's reputation is a difficult task. A company's reputation is built on the opinions of hundreds or even thousands of individuals. So whose opinions need to be influenced? Historically, companies concentrated their attention on influencing the opinions of shareholders. During the 1990s their attention turned also to customers and to employees, who began to be seen as the custodians of corporate brand and reputation. Recently, international companies have learned to their cost that the views of all of a company's major stakeholders – employees, customers, shareholders and investors, directors, the local community, suppliers – can at different times have an important impact on their reputation.

Disentangling stakeholders

Many people can have several stakeholder relationships with a company. For example, an executive director will also be an employee and may be a customer of it, as well as living in the community in which the company is located.

People not only have more than one stakeholder relationship with a company, they also have different expectations for different relationships. For example, the situation outlined in *Different stakeholders, different experiences* is typical of one situation many companies large and small find themselves in. It formed part of the market research for the National Forum.

Different stakeholders, different experiences

A small, private bus company is losing money. The company has a good reputation with its local community because it gives good service at low prices, it employs local people and in the past did not cut jobs when business was poor.

Now, however, the company must cut costs to keep the same level of profits for the owners. The owners are also the directors of the company and they live locally.

What in your experience as a customer/employee/director/investor/supplier/member of the wider community is the action most businesses take when faced with this situation?

A: Keep profits at the same level by cutting spending with suppliers, cutting jobs, and reducing the number of buses
B: Try to get more customers and reduce some costs, so that profits are reduced but jobs are not cut
C: Make cuts everywhere, to profits, jobs, some costs, and reduce the number of buses
D: Sell the business

Separate interviews were conducted with a representative random sample of each stakeholder group. The experience of private investors and directors is that companies would more often chose option B than the other options. The experience of suppliers and customers is that option C is most common. Employees, professional investors and members of the community most often experience companies pursuing option A.

Overall the National Forum market research showed that in the UK it is as members of the community that people have their highest expectations of business. For example, Monsanto suffered when it sought to introduce genetically modified foods without demonstrating that it had considered the views of members of the community. Marks and Spencer, already reeling from lacklustre performance, was hurt by what was perceived to be an excessively harsh decision to end without warning its long-standing contractual arrangements with suppliers such as William Baird. Barclays bank damaged its reputation when it announced the closure of rural branches and introduced charges for use of its automatic teller machines (ATMs) by non-customers, all at the time it was running an advertising campaign about how big the bank was.

Aligning core purposes and values with the brand

Just as keyhole surgery is replacing some major invasive surgical techniques, so too are businesses developing more subtle ways to align their core purposes and values with their brand. A sustainable reputation is built from the inside out by aligning the organisation's deep-rooted purposes and values with every aspect of its conduct and operations that combine to create its brand.

Most people's expectations of an organisation are managed through its brand. The company's brand is communicated through its people and products, its dress code and packaging, its premises and website. When the brand communicates the purposes and values of the business, people's expectations of the company's products or services will be matched or exceeded by their experiences.

If people's experiences of a company are to measure up to their expectations then the brand should be the external manifestation of the core purposes and values. However, the relationship between the two is not direct. What translates the inner purposes and values into what a brand stands for is a company's know-how and its plans, policies and processes. Any strategy to align the company's brand with its core purposes and values needs to address all four levels of Figure 7.1.

The first layer above the core purposes is know-how, which is crucial in the new economy. A company has four types of know-how spread among its employees and in some cases in documents and computer systems.

- **Technical and professional:** such as the software and systems knowledge that so many companies need today or the professional knowledge of professional service firms such as lawyers, accountants and surveyors.
- **Customers and clients:** such as retailers' knowledge of the

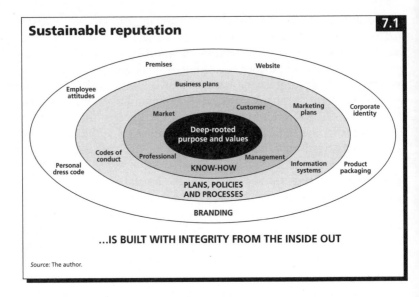

Sustainable reputation 7.1

...IS BUILT WITH INTEGRITY FROM THE INSIDE OUT

Source: The author.

detailed buying habits and interests of customers or a professional service firm's client knowledge.

◪ **Market:** competition, pricing, new entrants, new products and services.

◪ **Management skills and capability:** enterprise, initiative, teamwork and ethical fitness (see Chapter 4) can take years to develop in a workforce. Without them companies will find it difficult to adapt to change and align their brands with their purposes and values.

Companies can no longer rely on a periodic strategic review at board level. Employees need to be constantly collecting information, monitoring changes and adapting their part of the business to changes in the marketplace. This is especially true in professional services organisations and new-economy companies, which must grapple with and adapt swiftly to rapid market changes.

The second layer of plans, policies and procedures is well described in management literature. The outer layer of branding now includes any websites a company may have as well as all the other parts of the business through which the customer, investor and wider community may come into contact with the company.

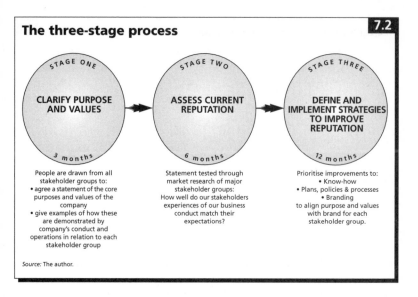

The three-stage process `7.2`

STAGE ONE

CLARIFY PURPOSE AND VALUES

3 months

People are drawn from all stakeholder groups to:
• agree a statement of the core purposes and values of the company
• give examples of how these are demonstrated by company's conduct and operations in relation to each stakeholder group

STAGE TWO

ASSESS CURRENT REPUTATION

6 months

Statement tested through market research of major stakeholder groups:
How well do our stakeholders experiences of our business conduct match their expectations?

STAGE THREE

DEFINE AND IMPLEMENT STRATEGIES TO IMPROVE REPUTATION

12 months

Prioritise improvements to:
• Know-how
• Plans, policies & processes
• Branding
to align purpose and values with brand for each stakeholder group.

Source: The author.

Three steps to an inside-out approach

Any business needs to go through three stages (see Figure 7.2).

1 Clarify purposes and values in relation to business operations and conduct.
2 Assess current reputation against purposes and values.
3 Define and implement strategies to improve reputation.

The remainder of this section describes these three stages in more detail and refers to research conducted by National Forum on the purposes and values of business. It also shows how this was used by Catering & Allied to review and improve its reputation.

Clarifying purposes and values

The objective of this process is to agree a statement of the purposes and values of the company together with typical situations of the company's day-to-day operations that illustrate their purpose and values in action.

Figure 7.3 summarises a typical process that might involve from 20 to 200 people depending on the size of the company. The rest of this section explains the process in more detail.

The conclusions from the UK's 1999 National Forum on purposes and

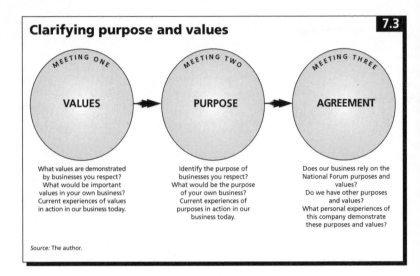

Clarifying purpose and values 7.3

MEETING ONE — **VALUES**
MEETING TWO — **PURPOSE**
MEETING THREE — **AGREEMENT**

What values are demonstrated by businesses you respect? What would be important values in your own business? Current experiences of values in action in our business today.

Identify the purpose of businesses you respect? What would be the purpose of your own business? Current experiences of purposes in action in our business today.

Does our business rely on the National Forum purposes and values? Do we have other purposes and values? What personal experiences of this company demonstrate these purposes and values?

Source: The author.

values provide all businesses with a useful common starting point. At the most fundamental level, the Forum found that people expect businesses to have three core purposes.

- **To trade profitably** – by creating profits for shareholders, repaying debt and providing cash for future investment in the business.
- **To reward enterprise** – by producing and supplying goods and services at prices people can afford and are willing to pay.
- **To reward effort** – by paying employees for their contribution to business success, and by creating and providing jobs both directly and indirectly.

But people also expect businesses to take into account the interests of the wider community and the following values.

- **Honesty** – telling the truth, integrity, transparency, openness, complying with standards, regulations and the law, keeping agreements both legally and in the spirit of the agreement.
- **Trust** – being reliable and dependable, and establishing relationships of mutual trust with stakeholders.
- **Respect** – taking other people's points of view seriously, valuing people, caring, co-operating and respecting people's dignity.
- **Responsibility** – taking responsibility for its actions, products and

so on, and reacting positively when they are found to be lacking.
- **Fairness** – acting justly and helpfully, rather than according to the letter of the law.
- **Innovation** – thinking up new ways of doing things better for the benefit of stakeholders as a whole.

The above list will help companies clarify their purposes and values, but what matters is how they put them into practice. The National Forum participants identified over 120 examples of business operations and conduct that demonstrated these purposes and values. These were boiled down to 24 typical situations (three or four for each stakeholder group and one generic to all) that were common to most businesses. These provide a starting point for organisations to identify typical situations through which they can demonstrate their purposes and values to their stakeholders.

Companies involved in the National Forum found that the process of involving small groups made up of stakeholders from all walks of life had a number of benefits, including:

- improving staff and director development in ethical thinking;
- improving training and education on a company's core purposes and values;
- bringing a greater awareness and understanding of stakeholders' expectations, experience of the business and closer personal relationships;
- sending a positive message to stakeholders that a company wants to involve them in both defining and achieving its core purposes and values.

Assessing current reputation
The National Forum developed a simple market research tool that can be adapted for any business to assess its current reputation (see *Catering & Allied assesses its reputation*). It has two main characteristics:

- It is inclusive – representative samples are taken from each of the six major stakeholder groups: customers, employees, suppliers, directors, shareholders and the community.
- It translates purposes and values into action – the measures are based on individual responses to everyday situations familiar to each stakeholder group.

Catering & Allied assesses its reputation

Catering & Allied was at the time (1999) a medium sized company providing contracted out catering services to companies and other organisations. In all they had 87 units in 61 different client companies, employed 1065 people of whom 3 were both directors and shareholders and 1 was only a director. All the sample sizes were small, the minimum possible for statistically significant results. In the case of directors and shareholders, almost everyone was interviewed. It proved too difficult to identify and interview a sample from the wider community.

This was how Catering & Allied adapted one National Forum market research question to ask its customers about its own business.

National Forum market research question
You went to look at used cars in a local garage. You put down a deposit on one car so that the salesman would hold it for you, and you would pay the full amount when you collected the car. Two weeks later you changed your mind and called the garage to ask for your money back.

One salesman said that you couldn't have the deposit back because you had agreed to buy that car. You called again, and another salesman said there was no problem, and you could have your deposit back.

You went to collect your deposit but then you were told that you couldn't have your deposit back because the deposit meant you had agreed to buy the car, and you must pay the rest of the price of the car in 28 days. You complained to the garage owner.

Q1 Now I'd like you to imagine that you were the garage owner. Which of these four actions would you take?

Q2 In your experience as a customer of any kind of business, which action would be most likely in this type of situation?

1   Do not give back the deposit and try to get the customer to pay in full for the car.
2   Repay the deposit.
3   Offer to carry over the deposit to another car.
4   Pay back half of the customer's deposit and discipline the sales staff.

Catering and Allied adaptation of market research question
The Commercial Manager of a contract catering company has just signed a contract with a new client. A week later the client has called to say he has had second thoughts about the cost of the contract and would like to cancel. The Commercial Manager has already made commitments for increased business from several suppliers. There is a penalty clause in the contract, equivalent to the cost of two months' service, that the Commercial Manager has the right to invoke.

Q1 Now I'd like you to imagine that you were the head of Catering and Allied. Which of these four actions would you take?

Q2 In your experience as a customer of Catering and Allied, which action would be most likely in this type of situation?

1 Inform the client that the penalty clause will be invoked in order to make good any costs already incurred to suppliers.
2 Cancel the contract.
3 Offer to defer the start of the contract so that the client can sort out the contract financing.
4 Cancel the contract but request payment of half the penalty payment.

Many companies now conduct customer and employee surveys at regular intervals. These can usefully be adapted to measure the purposes and values a company is communicating, but they need to be extended to measure all stakeholder relationships. Moreover, the measures need to probe beyond people's opinions to uncover their relevant experience. For the National Forum, this was achieved by designing a measure that matched experiences with expectations:

- How each stakeholder group **experiences** the company's brand through its operations and conduct in everyday situations.
- How close these experiences are to what those same groups **expect** the company to do in the same situations.

The difference between them is a measure of corporate reputation:

Reputation = Experiences − Expectations

The market research tool involves a short questionnaire which asks the interviewee to consider four situations and in each case to select from a choice of answers which comes closest to describing:

1 What action they would take if they ran the company (**expectation**)
2 What action was, in their experience, most likely (**experience**)

Each stakeholder group is asked to consider situations which are typical for their type of relationship with the company.

National Opinion Polls, a market research firm, interviewed representative samples of six stakeholder groups: employees, customers, suppliers, directors, investors and the wider community. In total, over 2,000 interviews were conducted during late 1999.

The results from the National Forum market research can be used as a benchmark against which companies can measure their own reputation compared with the reputation of business in general in Britain.

Defining and implementing strategies to improve reputation

The strategy for aligning the purposes and values with the brand needs to start with analysing what aspects of an organisation's conduct and operations have the most direct impact on priority stakeholder groups, and what changes to its conduct and operations might communicate the purposes and values most effectively.

Any strategy should involve directors and employees in identifying what needs to change. The National Forum questionnaires and market research methods provide organisations with a way of measuring how well their purposes and values are being communicated through their day to day operations to each of their stakeholder groups. From this the priorities for action can be drawn up and a strategy developed.

The process of recognising the different views and expectations of each stakeholder group can help change the attitudes and behaviour of staff and directors, and thereby the management knowledge of the business. However, this will need to be supported by policies and codes that reinforce the attitudes and behaviour the company wants to encourage. Figure 7.1 provided a conceptual framework for considering each level of the business to ensure that nothing is overlooked. *Inside-out changes* (below) illustrates how the inside-out approach might look in practice.

Inside-out changes

A professional firm wishes to grow from 20 to 50 partners while also building a sustainable reputation for value for money and client service (respect, trust, innovation). This will require changes at all levels. One important change is to encourage partners to work more in teams with each other, assistants and other professionals. Typically, partners in a small firm are used to working on transactions alone or with one other. Here are a few examples of what the change strategy will involve from the "inside out".

Management know-how
Partners will need to learn how to work in teams: delegating work to assistants, sharing clients with other partners. Team-building workshops will be essential as well as opportunities to practise and develop their skills.

Plans, policies and processes
- Information systems: typically, partner management information will require changes from reporting individual partners' billing performance to reporting team performance, and firm-wide client invoicing.
- Appraisal and reward systems: partners will be increasingly rewarded on their ability to build a team and the performance of the whole team. This will be integrated into any appraisal system and reflected in any reward system.

Branding
Firm literature will emphasise teamwork and place less emphasis on full partner involvement in all transactions.

Benchmarking

Catering & Allied measured up well to the national benchmark, scoring higher than the benchmark overall. On closer analysis of the scores for each stakeholder group it was clear that although they were exceeding their customers' expectations their reputation with other stakeholders needed to improve. Based on these and other findings the company drew up a strategy to improve its reputation. The managing director described how the results of the benchmarking process were used to embark upon a radical process of change:

The results of the survey in many ways held no surprises. In fact they confirmed what we already knew. We already had a strong culture and the business was guided by straightforward and simple philosophies. What we had never really examined was the effectiveness of these philosophies in the business context, and the benchmarking enabled us to do that.

Our research gave us the means to test the temperature of our business from all angles.

Client satisfaction has always been the driving force behind the business, and we discovered that this was reflected in the research results. Our clients experience scores higher than their expectations. The point of learning for us was that the continual search for client satisfaction often had the effect of overlooking equally important areas of the business, and in some cases using this philosophy as an excuse to avoid difficult decisions.

What we found was that all of the elements of our business examined by the research needed equal attention. We had to learn to attend to the needs of all of our stakeholders if we were to deliver a more sustainable business. In essence we had to find new ways of doing the same things.

If we could bring delight to our clients, why couldn't we do the same for our suppliers? The research demonstrated to us that all of the needs of our stakeholders formed a kind of business jigsaw, all the components of which had to slot together. We had never really considered the business in that way.

What sometimes was seen to conflict with our core philosophies could now be challenged more effectively and in a positive and creative manner. One example of this was the reappraisal of our dealings with our suppliers. Previously, the need to deliver flexible solutions to our clients meant that our people on site had the option to use whatever suppliers they chose. We knew that to become more profitable we had to reduce our supplier base.

We now knew that an inclusive approach was likely to deliver greater benefits, and armed with the results from the research, we were able to put in place a process which involved a wide range of stakeholders, principally our *people, our clients, our suppliers, and even some shareholders. We created focus groups made up of representatives from the above groups and gave each group the challenge of finding solutions to the problem.*

The result was to reduce the pain of the exercise, and to increase dramatically the speed at which it was carried out. Within eight weeks we had halved our supplier base. Those who lost business with us understood the reasons why, and had been fully involved in the selection process. They respected us for it. Our managers and chefs had driven the exercise and were fully committed to it. They dealt with issues and problems that subsequently arose. Our clients were satisfied that food and service quality would not suffer as a result. The suppliers who remained were paid more promptly, since there was now less administration. Ultimately, our profits almost doubled.

I doubt if traditional thinking would have delivered comparable results. The benefit of the benchmarking research has been to allow the organisation to carry out an audit of its conscience and of its practices, to take stock and refocus on those parts of the business that are often ignored. It helped create a new way of thinking and from a really practical perspective gave us some of the means to move the business in a new direction.

Conclusion

When a business is clear about its core purposes and values and aligns its brand with them it will be more likely to:

- attract and keep talented people;
- reduce inefficiency and stress caused by conflicting messages about purposes and values and brands;
- attract and retain clients and customers who are delighted by their expectations being exceeded by the organisation's everyday conduct and operations;
- attract and keep suppliers who deliver goods and services to the same quality and standards.

3

THE OUTSIDE WORLD

8 New ethical frontiers in emerging markets

Jane Nelson and Frances House

GLOBALISATION AND THE END OF THE COLD WAR HAVE TAKEN COMPANIES
INTO A WIDER RANGE OF COUNTRIES, SOME OF WHICH HAVE FRAGILE
SOCIAL STRUCTURES AND LIMITED EXPERIENCE OF THE WORKING OF A
MARKET ECONOMY ... THAT MEANS WORKING IN SOME COMPLEX AREAS: IN
SOUTHERN AFRICA, IN AREAS BLIGHTED BY AIDS; IN ANGOLA, A COUNTRY
BESET BY CIVIL WAR FOR 40 YEARS; IN COLOMBIA, A COUNTRY TRYING TO
ESCAPE THE GRIP OF ORGANISED CRIME AND THE IMPACT OF THE DRUG
TRADE; AND IN RUSSIA, A COUNTRY STILL COMING TO TERMS WITH
TRANSITION TO A MARKET-BASED ECONOMY AND LACKING REAL
ENFORCEMENT MECHANISMS FOR THEIR LAWS ... IF GLOBALISATION MARKS
THE END OF SOVEREIGNTY FOR NATIONAL GOVERNMENTS IT SHOULD ALSO
EQUALLY END ANY SENSE OF SPLENDID ISOLATION WHICH EXISTS IN THE
CORPORATE WORLD.

Sir John Browne, CEO, BP

MANY CHAPTERS IN this book discuss how managers must strike a
delicate balance between opportunity and risk as they manage
the ethical dimensions of their businesses. Emerging markets illustrate
this balancing act most starkly. The potential gains are huge, yet the
risks to company reputation are as great. Previous chapters have
examined how companies can create ethical cultures and ethically fit
individuals. The importance of such strategies becomes glaringly
evident in emerging markets, especially those with a high incidence of
human rights abuses and political or economic corruption. Careless
decisions by managers, or even a simple failure to gather more
information, may suddenly embroil a company in accusations of
propping up a corrupt foreign government or contributing to regional
conflicts.

These issues are relevant to any company that operates
internationally. Dramatic political changes in the past decade, notably
in former communist countries, has meant that most of the world is
now "open for business", giving companies access to over 3.5 billion

potential new customers. Investment in these new markets has soared – capital flows to emerging markets have increased sixfold since 1990 to reach over $250 billion. Foreign investment in the world's 44 poorest countries has also increased, from an annual average of under $1 billion between 1987 and 1992 to nearly $3 billion in 1998. The World Bank estimates that the European Union's share of emerging markets in world trade could grow from today's figure of 25% to more than 50% by 2020.

Playing by whose rules?

Profoundly different working conditions, and an absence of firm ground rules, mean that emerging markets present a host of often unfamiliar risks and challenges. Some examples are as follows.

- Flimsy legal frameworks and governance structure – national or local political authorities may simply lack the resources and administrative capabilities to uphold the law, or sizeable numbers of a country's citizens may dispute their legitimacy.
- Authoritarian regimes.
- Serious inequities in the distribution of resources and livelihood opportunities.
- A lack of independent systems of law, justice and mediation.
- High levels of bribery and corruption.
- Human rights violations.
- Unaccountable or undisciplined security forces.
- State-sponsored or condoned human rights abuses, terrorism or corruption.
- Strict press controls.
- Aggressive local leadership factions.
- Local antagonism, possibly stemming from a belief that foreign companies plunder natural resources or deflect profits away from local communities to foreign investors or unpopular national organisations, groups or individuals.

Ignoring these risks and challenges is not an option. Companies are increasingly under the spotlight in both the emerging market or "host" country and internationally, thanks to activist groups, the media, consumers and even a growing number of investors. They must be seen to operate in an ethical and accountable manner. This requires companies to apply the same principles and operating standards for managing their economic, social and environmental impacts as they do in OECD countries, especially concerning:

- standards of corporate governance;
- efforts to prevent bribery and corruption;
- adherence to international conventions on human rights, labour rights and the environment.

Nowhere to hide

A further spur to companies to manage the ethical risks of operation in emerging markets is ever toughening international and national law.

Until recently, the major worry for companies involved in questionable activities abroad was the damage to their corporate or brand reputations. Changes to international law now mean that companies may be sued at home for offences committed abroad. In Britain, for example, the law lords ruled in July 2000 that compensation claims by 3,000 South African employees of a subsidiary of Cape plc who are suffering from asbestosis could be heard in the UK given the lack of legal aid provision in South Africa, thus opening the door for subsidiaries of UK companies to be held accountable for their operations abroad. In the same year in the United States activist lawyers brought a civil lawsuit on the behalf of 12 Burmese farmers against Unocal, an American oil company. The plaintiffs sought $1 billion from Unocal for abuses of their human rights by the Burmese troops responsible for safeguarding the company's pipeline, which it owned jointly with another company. The premise of this civil action was that American companies should be legally responsible for their own behaviour overseas and also that of a joint-venture partner, including foreign companies and state owned enterprises.

There has been a marked increase in the risk of transboundary litigation, particularly for companies accused of human rights abuses or complicity in such abuses. The 1948 UN Universal Declaration on Human Rights calls on "every individual and every organ of society" to play its part in securing the observance of these rights. Companies that have violated universal standards have found, to their cost, that society condemns them.

The real costs of such lawsuits can include damage to the corporate or brand reputation and the resulting impact on employee recruitment and retention, consumer loyalty, risk ratings and even share price. More tangible costs are the on-the-ground costs of risk management and material losses where company property is destroyed. In Colombia, for example, pipelines managed by Western oil companies in joint ventures with EcoPetrol, Colombia's state-owned oil company, are regularly blown up.

These costs are likely to be higher for investors in the extractive, infrastructure and heavy industry sectors, for example, than for investors in consumer goods, financial services and tourism companies. Companies in the former group have major long-term on-the-ground investments and active engagement in strategic (and hence conflict-sensitive) industries.

Examining the issues

The following sections illustrate the range of ethical issues that companies must grapple with in many emerging markets and how managing them involves many different players, an ever-changing plot and a more discerning and questioning audience. Just following the script is no longer an option: to survive and succeed foreign companies must be willing to write some of it for themselves. Perhaps the most important part of this process is simply to ask the right questions about the ethical dilemmas posed by emerging markets and to debate the scope of the company's responsibility for tackling the root causes of these issues.

In the often unstable situations in emerging markets, companies face a dual challenge.

- To take full responsibility for managing their own activities and interactions with society at the level of the individual enterprise, or micro-level.
- To address some of the structural challenges at the macro-level that make these locations prone to instability in the first place, preferably with other parties, such as government agencies and non-governmental organisations (NGOs).

Dealing with repressive and/or corrupt regimes

One of the most difficult choices for multinational companies is whether or how to deal with governments that are repressive, authoritarian or undemocratic (whether officially condemned by the UN or not). Such countries may be the targets of NGO and media campaigns, but multinational companies are legally free to invest in them. In such cases, the decision to invest, to remain or to disinvest, is a business decision, taken solely at the discretion of the company in question.

Burma/Myanmar is a current example: US oil companies Texaco, Amoco, Arco and Baker Hughes have withdrawn their investments, but Unocal has decided to stay, together with its French operating partner TotalfinaElf. UK-based Premier Oil was officially requested to disinvest by the British government in April 2000. This was not a legally binding demand, given that official economic sanctions against the country by the UK and other European governments are limited. The company has for now decided to remain invested, arguing: "We believe constructive engagement is more likely to bring progress in countries like Burma."

Many companies with brand reputations to protect have pulled out of Myanmar, notably Best Western, a hotels group, and Suzuki, a Japanese car maker. They have been particularly spurred by the Free Burma Coalition, an umbrella group of organisations working for freedom and democracy in Myanmar, and the imposition of US government sanctions on new investments by US companies. The risk to their reputation and the management costs of staying outweighed companies' assessments of the business benefits of staying.

The Coalition cites almost 30 major multinationals – including PepsiCo, Heineken, Carlsberg, Hewlett-Packard, Amoco, Texaco, Motorola and Seagram – that have divested from the country since 1992, in part as a response to its campaigning activities.

ETHICAL QUESTIONS

- Are we willing to deal with a repressive, authoritarian or undemocratic government?
- What are the ethical pros and cons of continuing to invest in, divesting from, exporting to or importing from this region?
- If we let ethical issues take priority over commercial interests, can we defend this position to our shareholders and stakeholders?

Benefiting from "war economies"

There has been a growing focus on the economic factors that sustain civil wars. Barter and cash-based trade in primary commodities is one way in which government and rebel factions alike fund their war efforts. The presence of primary commodity exports massively increases the risk of civil conflict in a country: diamonds from Angola, Sierra Leone and the Congo; oil from Angola and the Sudan; timber and rubber from Liberia; and opium from Myanmar and Afghanistan. There is also the long-standing example of the complex links between governments, state armies, rebel factions and drug barons in Latin America.

Illegal trade in these commodities can take many forms, for example:

- bartering between arms traders and local intermediaries who represent different warring interests;
- smuggling illegally sourced primary commodities, such as African "conflict" diamonds, across borders and then selling them on the world market through legal routes.

Even if the trade is legal along the entire value chain, it may enable governments to fund conflict. Angola, for example, has been embroiled in civil war since 1975. A high percentage of revenue from the trade in Angolan diamonds, which has been both illicit and official, has funded the UNITA rebel movement. Meanwhile, revenue from official oil production is funding Angolan government forces. Both products end up in Western markets through value chains that include well-known multinational companies and banks, all operating legally.

Diamond companies have been criticised for insufficiently controlling the purchase of diamonds that have been smuggled illegally from Angola and are then sold through legal channels on the world market. Oil companies and banks have been criticised for not being proactive enough in influencing the Angolan government to be more transparent and accountable about the way it uses its oil revenue. The situation is complicated further by the fact that there are Angolans on both the government and rebel sides cutting deals with each other.

In October 1999, a group of four European NGOs launched an international campaign, *Fatal transactions*, to promote more vigilant and responsible practices in the diamond industry. In December 1999, Global Witness launched a linked report and campaign, *Crude awakening*, aimed at the banks and oil companies operating in Angola. In September 1999, Human Rights Watch also set out recommendations for oil and diamond companies in its report *Angola unravels*. As a result of these three campaigns, some major investors have started to review their activities in "war economies" and there have been some fundamental improvements in the way the global diamond industry operates, spearheaded by De Beers, a mining company.

ETHICAL QUESTIONS
- Are our activities helping to fund and sustain war economies?
- If so, what can we do about it?

◾ Do we feel that it is our responsibility to mitigate the negative impact of our involvement?
◾ If so, what potential is there for collective action within the war economy in question and internationally to have a more positive impact?

Managing security arrangements

How can companies handle the security of their employees and physical assets in emerging economies where they may be at risk from, say, the activities of warring military groups, organised crime or local communities that have grievances against outside investment?

Companies operating in unstable emerging markets risk:

◾ being caught in the middle of conflict between opposing groups;
◾ employees or contractors being kidnapped (to extort money, to make political gestures, to achieve military advances, to gain media attention or to air grievances against the company or government);
◾ having their operations sabotaged by guerrilla groups or local community activists;
◾ armed robbery or hijacks.

Companies must be able to respond effectively to such events. But they may not be able to rely on the local security services, which may lack the resources or skills to do the job and may even be part of the problem. For example, they may be guilty of human rights violations against the local population.

This has contributed to a big increase in the "privatisation" of security. But some of these private security forces have themselves used violent and controversial methods. It is argued that the trend towards privatisation has also encouraged the growth of unauthorised militias, local warlords, narco-guerrillas and mercenaries.

Shell and BP Amoco are among a small number of companies that have developed company-wide guidelines and compliance systems for their employees and contractors for the management of security services. Prompted in part by adverse public reaction to allegations of their complicity in human rights violations in Nigeria and Colombia respectively, both companies have revised their "rules of engagement" with security forces to include UN frameworks and to incorporate feedback from NGOs such as Amnesty International and Human Rights

Watch. Shell now reports publicly on how its own operations, joint ventures and contractor firms are complying with its security guidelines.

In 1999, BP Amoco, which had been criticised about the socio-economic and environmental impacts of its investment and security arrangements in the Casanare region of Colombia, engaged in an intensive dialogue with a group of UK-based development NGOS (CAFOD, Christian Aid, Catholic Institute for International Relations, Oxfam UK, Save the Children Fund UK). It has also established a framework by which its employees in Colombia, Azerbaijan and Algeria can learn from each other's experiences and practices in the area of security.

ETHICAL QUESTIONS

- ◼ Should we develop policies, operating standards, monitoring and accountability procedures when hiring private security forces?
- ◼ How do we ensure that the activities of these private forces do not exacerbate human rights violations or sustain violent conflict, but serve only to protect against, or stabilise or resolve, the violence?
- ◼ At the same time, how can we comply with international human rights standards?
- ◼ Should we get involved with international efforts to draft principles and guidelines for the use of security forces by companies with regard to human rights standards? (For example, the US State Department, the UK Foreign and Commonwealth Office launched in December 2000 a set of voluntary guidelines on security and human rights for companies in the extractive sector. These were drawn up by the two governments and a number of UK and US-based extractive companies and NGOS.)

Dealing with corruption

Corruption, which is covered in detail in Chapter 9, often flourishes where there is bad governance, violent conflict or where state control and regulations have broken down.

ETHICAL QUESTIONS

- ◼ At what level do we tackle corruption? Should we engage in and influence public policy debate on corruption, and help to build the necessary enabling frameworks to tackle it at local, national and international levels?
- ◼ Should we get involved with local forums and pacts between

major companies and agree to abide by common, voluntary rules and guidelines?
- ◪ Should we establish anti-corruption agreements with our business partners?
- ◪ Should we prioritise our own activities? How should we implement and monitor anti-corruption policies in all our business operations?

Addressing land rights and indigenous peoples' rights

The growth of oil and gas exploration, production and mining in remote regions has given rise to demands that companies take account of indigenous claims to land and resources as an integral part of the project planning process.

The past few years have seen complex negotiations over land and treaty rights, control of mineral development, profit sharing and compensation arrangements. A significant number of countries have amended their laws and policies on indigenous issues. New declarations, conventions, policy guidelines for multilateral financial institutions and proposed codes of conduct for corporations present new operational challenges for companies.

Although companies like Shell may have adopted policies on indigenous peoples in recent years, the general challenge lies in their implementation. For a multinational company, a constructive and consistent approach to issues involving indigenous peoples can reap dividends in terms of reputation, good community relations and the smooth operation of a project.

The experience of WMC Resources, an Australian-based minerals company, at Tampakaen in the Philippines provides insights into how companies can avoid a clash of cultures and develop relationships of mutual respect with indigenous peoples.

The site of WMC's exploration activities is home to some 2,300 people belonging to five indigenous Bla'an communities, which have traditionally engaged in hunting and slash-and-burn agriculture. The history of Bla'an interaction with logging companies is littered with broken promises. Some Bla'an formed armed groups to combat the military, and their successful resistance led to an amnesty being issued during the Aquino presidency. WMC had to contend with a deep-seated mistrust of outsiders among the Bla'an – the legacy of progressive encroachment by settlers and logging companies.

Under the terms of a formal agreement with the Philippines

government, wmc is obliged to "recognise and respect the rights, customs and traditions of indigenous tribal peoples". This is broadly consistent with the indigenous peoples policy that the company adopted in 1995, the first to be produced by a mining company.

After early consultation with tribal leaders, in 1994 and 1995 the company committed itself to supporting Bla'an ancestral domain claims. Ethnographic and archaeological records were subsequently prepared and the boundaries of traditional territories mapped. The government then awarded certificates of ancestral domain, recognising Bla'an rights to occupy and use the land.

ETHICAL QUESTIONS

◪ Do we genuinely respect and acknowledge the land rights of indigenous people, or do we simply pay lip service?
◪ Are we aware of national and international laws and policies?
◪ Is this issue an integral part of our project planning process?
◪ Should we create a code of conduct and how do we monitor the way our staff treat indigenous people and negotiate with them during a project?

Ensuring labour rights

Emerging markets often present problems regarding barriers to labour rights, and companies should take the conventions of the International Labour Organisation (ILO) as their starting point for evaluating their particular situation.

Freedom of association is enshrined in the Universal Declaration of Human Rights and two ILO conventions. In countries such as China and Vietnam, free trade union activity is not permitted and in others it is seen as a threat to corporate and national competitiveness. The International Confederation of Free Trade Unions (ICFTU) has estimated that in 1998 some 2,000 union activists were killed or tortured by the state.

Child labour is an emotive issue, and one of great complexity. The UN Convention on the Rights of the Child, the most widely ratified human rights treaty to date, asserts: "The child has the right to be protected from work that threatens his or her health, education or development. The State shall set minimum ages for employment and regulate working conditions." Two ILO conventions also define what constitutes acceptable ages and conditions for employment, and a new convention aims to prohibit and immediately eliminate the worst forms of child labour, including slavery, trafficking, prostitution and pornography.

Debate continues between those who take an absolutist approach to abolishing all forms of child labour and those who believe that access to work can be an economic necessity for children and their families. The latter focus their efforts on abolishing exploitative labour and developing improved access to education and compensating for lost earnings.

Establishing standards for safe and decent working conditions remains a focus of the ILO's work. A company's influence over working conditions lessens the lower the degree of direct control it has over its operations and the longer its supply chain. As Chapter 10 makes clear, companies are increasingly held responsible for violations along their supply chains and are well advised to have some sort of monitoring process in place.

Bonded labour, one of the oldest forms of slavery, is illegal almost everywhere yet still affects millions of adults and children and migrant workers. Types of bonded labour are found in many places, but it is perhaps most common in India, Pakistan and Nepal, where it has its roots in the caste system and in feudal agriculture relationships.

Companies can be involved in forced labour by association when workers are forced by the state to do particular jobs. For example, any company operating in Myanmar may find itself benefiting indirectly from state forced labour that has been used on infrastructure projects. In 1999, member governments of the ILO adopted a resolution citing the country for consistent violations of the Forced Labour Convention.

Companies may not be aware that components of products they source from abroad may have been produced by unremunerated captive or prison labour. It is difficult if not impossible to monitor working conditions in detention, but organisations such as Amnesty International and Human Rights Watch have documented abusive forms of captive labour in certain countries.

ETHICAL QUESTIONS

- ◪ At what levels are we prepared to tackle labour rights? Are we prepared to raise concerns with relevant government officials through diplomacy or more aggressive lobbying?
- ◪ Do we want to establish partnerships with NGOs and labour organisations?
- ◪ If union activity is illegal, are we prepared to explore opportunities for an alternative employee representation system?
- ◪ Are we ensuring the safety of employee and union representatives where appropriate?

■ Should we create some company principles on labour rights and incorporate these into our contracts with joint-venture partners and subcontractors?

■ Are we willing to inform employees of their rights and to monitor standards and procedures in all our operations?

The way forward

Any business that wishes to take an active stance on ethical issues in emerging markets can do the following four things.

Make a strategic commitment

A small but growing number of companies are establishing policy statements, principles and operating guidelines on issues such as human rights, anti-corruption measurements, security arrangements, labour conditions, indigenous people, the environment and so on.

In some companies, these are incorporated into statements of General Business Principles. In others, they are addressed in separate guidelines. Increasingly, both approaches are used, with general commitments to good practice and then more detailed operational procedures on complex issues. During 1999 and 2000, for example, Shell, BP Amoco, Rio Tinto, BT, Premier Oil, Nokia, Novo Nordisk, Norsk Hydro and Statoil incorporated explicit statements on human rights into their business principles or policy statements.

Engage in dialogue and consultation

As noted in other chapters, businesses must engage in regular dialogue and consultation with stakeholders to ensure that they understand what the company is trying to achieve and the practical and strategic constraints that it faces. This is especially important for companies operating in emerging markets, where those with whom the dialogue needs to take pace include government, intergovernmental agencies, and local and international NGOs. In countries run by repressive or corrupt regimes, companies have to balance working with government officials when appropriate and taking a stand against them, in public or in private, when necessary.

NGOs and communities can present unfamiliar challenges. To be successful in working with them companies need to:

■ identify the right people and organisations to engage with;
■ overcome any legacies of mistrust and ignorance on both sides;

◾ develop frameworks and consultation skills that allow for genuine two-way dialogue as against one-way public relations and campaigning;
◾ make sure the process is continuous and not just a one-off exercise.

These activities are time-consuming and resource-intensive. Many companies are reluctant to allow outsiders, especially NGOs, into the process. It takes time to develop a culture within a company and among business partners that supports such engagement. The most successful examples have occurred when an individual from a company and an individual from a NGO have built a personal relationship of trust. Even so, these individuals can still struggle to get their organisations or communities fully behind them.

Do it with others

Working with partners and encouraging collective action makes a big difference. Collaboration involving business, government and civil organisations is comparatively common, but there are a growing number of "business in society" coalitions of companies that have been established to address specific social, economic, environmental or political issues. Examples include the National Business Initiative in South Africa, the Philippines Business for Social Progress, Business for Social Responsibility in the United States and the Instituto Ethos in Brazil.

Collective action is usually the most realistic option for a company operating in a politically sensitive environment. This is especially the case when dealing with structural issues; for example, trying to bring a reduction in violence or influencing public policy reform in areas such as human rights, corruption, labour standards and state security systems. It can also be an effective structure for mobilising resources and leveraging different skills and capacities for practical projects, in areas such as education, health, civic institution-building and infrastructure development.

Evaluate and account

In broad terms, corporate accountability has two main components.

◾ A company's ability and willingness to understand, manage, measure and verify the positive and negative social, economic and environmental impacts of its operations.

■ The ability and willingness to report on these impacts and engage in dialogue with a growing number of stakeholders, ranging from shareholders to local communities.

This requires managers to develop appropriate internal skills and competencies to tackle each of these areas. It also requires an external enabling framework, ranging from regulations and voluntary codes of conduct to stakeholder pressure and support services, to ensure that companies have the necessary incentives and parameters to undertake the process in the first place (see Chapter 12).

Conclusion

The integration of ethics into business is a question of values and leadership. It is in emerging markets that companies are most likely to find that there is a conflict between the values and standards they espouse and local values and standards. Because of this, it is in emerging markets that strong, clear and supportive leadership is most necessary if companies are to maintain their values and standards and make a difference.

9 Corruption

George Moody-Stuart

CORRUPTION CAN UNDO EVERYTHING ELSE WE ARE TRYING TO DO.
Dr Norman Borlaug, Nobel Peace Prize winner

CORRUPTION IS DEFINED by Transparency International[1] as "the misuse of public power for private gain". It takes many forms and can be intensely damaging. Research has found that in countries with a lot of corruption less of their GDP goes into investment and they have lower growth rates. They also invest less in education, thereby reducing their human capital, and they attract less foreign direct investment.

Let us start by considering two situations that might arise at any time in one of many countries.

- In the presidential palace, an executive decision is taken. "We must postpone the hospital building programme," says the president, "because the defence needs of the republic are of paramount importance. Instead we shall buy three fighter aircraft. These, I understand, will cost us about $100m."
- A few miles away, an official in the telecommunications department is talking to a newly arrived expatriate resident. "I am afraid that there is several weeks' delay in getting a telephone line, sir; but if you like to call my brother on this number" – passing a slip of paper – "he should be able to help."

These two examples are taken from opposite ends of the corruption scale, sometimes described as "grand" and "petty" corruption. The first may put $10m into the president's offshore bank account; the second may put $100 into the official's back pocket.

There is no clear-cut and universal dividing line between grand corruption, as practised by senior officials, government ministers and heads of state, and petty corruption, which is typically the realm of customs clerks, immigration officers and other low-paid officials. However, it is useful to recognise their different characteristics. Grand corruption is about the distortion of decision-making in matters of economic significance. Petty corruption is often about the removal of bureaucratic delays – hence the terms "facilitation payment" and "speed money", paying people to do faster what they have already been paid to do – although it is not always as simple as that.

A distinction must also be made between international (or offshore) corruption and domestic corruption. In the former, more than one legal jurisdiction is involved, whereas the latter falls within the control of a single government. Grand corruption is usually international, because of its scale. Petty corruption is virtually always domestic, although the payer may not be a citizen, or even a resident, of the country concerned.

The Law Commission in the UK, among others, has recently argued that the distinction between the bribing of a public official and of a private person is no longer relevant. It is probably true to say that from the payer's point of view it is no more heinous to bribe, say, a local-government planning officer than the purchasing director of a privatised utility or, indeed, the buyer for a supermarket chain. However, there remains an argument that the public-sector official (or even someone performing a quasi-public function within a regulated industry) owes a duty to the public at large that is different in its nature from that owed by a private-sector employee to his company, its shareholders or its customers. This chapter focuses on corruption involving public officials rather than on corrupt transactions between individuals in the private sector.

How widespread is corruption?

Few, if any, countries can claim to be free of corruption, although its incidence varies tremendously from country to country. Transparency International's annual Corruption Perception Index (CPI) provides one measure. The most recent CPI ranked 99 countries on the basis of polls carried out by 17 different institutions, excluding any country for which at least three independent polls were not available. Scores were allotted from 10 to 0, with 10 indicating "very clean" and 0 "highly corrupt". The rankings and scores for the year 2000 are shown in Figure 9.1.

However, the CPI only considers the level of corruption within a country and does not attempt to take account of corrupt payments made by exporters to foreign officials. A new Bribe Payers Index, based on interviews carried out by Gallup International and published for the first time in 1999, ranked 19 leading exporters to developing countries and showed that companies from Sweden, Australia and Canada were the least likely to pay bribes, and those from Taiwan, South Korea and China were the most likely (see Figure 9.2).

Figure 9.1 **Corruption Perception Index, 2000**
   10 = "very clean", 0 = "highly corrupt"

1	Finland	10.0		Malawi	4.1
2	Denmark	9.8		Poland	4.1
3	New Zealand	9.4	48	South Korea	4.0
	Sweden	9.4	49	Brazil	3.9
5	Canada	9.2	50	Turkey	3.8
6	Iceland	9.1	51	Croatia	3.7
	Norway	9.1	52	Argentina	3.5
	Singapore	9.1		Bulgaria	3.5
9	Netherlands	8.9		Ghana	3.5
10	United Kingdom	8.7		Senegal	3.5
11	Luxembourg	8.6		Slovak Republic	3.5
	Switzerland	8.6	57	Latvia	3.4
13	Australia	8.3		Zambia	3.4
14	USA	7.8	59	Mexico	3.3
15	Austria	7.7	60	Colombia	3.2
	Hong Kong	7.7		Ethiopia	3.2
17	Germany	7.6		Thailand	3.2
18	Chile	7.4	63	China	3.1
19	Ireland	7.2		Egypt	3.1
20	Spain	7.0	65	Burkina Faso	3.0
21	France	6.7		Kazakhstan	3.0
22	Israel	6.6		Zimbabwe	3.0
23	Japan	6.4	68	Romania	2.9
	Portugal	6.4	69	India	2.8
25	Belgium	6.1		Philippines	2.8
26	Botswana	6.0	71	Bolivia	2.7
27	Estonia	5.7		Côte-d'Ivoire	2.7
28	Slovenia	5.5		Venezuela	2.7
	Taiwan	5.5	74	Ecuador	2.6
30	Costa Rica	5.4		Moldova	2.6
	Namibia	5.4	76	Armenia	2.5
32	Hungary	5.2		Tanzania	2.5
	Tunisia	5.2		Vietnam	2.5
34	South Africa	5.0	79	Uzbekistan	2.4
35	Greece	4.9	80	Uganda	2.3
36	Malaysia	4.8	81	Mozambique	2.2
37	Mauritius	4.7	82	Kenya	2.1
	Morocco	4.7		Russia	2.1
39	Italy	4.6	84	Cameroon	2.0
	Jordan	4.6	85	Angola	1.7
41	Peru	4.4		Indonesia	1.7
42	Czech Republic	4.3	87	Azerbaijan	1.5
43	Belarus	4.1		Ukraine	1.5
	El Salvador	4.1	89	Yugoslavia	1.3
	Lithuania	4.1	90	Nigeria	1.2

Source: Transparency International.

Figure 9.2 **Bribe Payers Index, 1999**
        In order of those least likely to pay bribes

1	Sweden	8.3
2	Australia	8.1
	Canada	8.1
4	Austria	7.8
5	Switzerland	7.7
6	Netherlands	7.4
7	United Kingdom	7.2
8	Belgium	6.8
9	Germany	6.2
	United States	6.2
11	Singapore	5.7
12	Spain	5.3
13	France	5.2
14	Japan	5.1
15	Malaysia	3.9
16	Italy	3.7
17	Taiwan	3.5
18	South Korea	3.4
19	China (including Hong Kong)	3.1

Source: Transparency International.

Grand corruption

The mechanism

Bribes are paid in order to win (or retain) business. It is, of course, in the interest of both the payer and the receiver of a bribe that it should be concealed as well as possible. Even in those countries where it is widely known that corruption is prevalent, the recipient of a bribe will not want any details to be known, and the payers of bribes, which are frequently large companies operating in many countries, have strong reasons to distance themselves from any questionable transactions. Hence the use of middlemen, often referred to as "representatives" or "agents".

There are, of course, many entirely legitimate tasks for a company's representative in an unfamiliar foreign country to perform. Advice may be needed on matters of law, finance, taxation, employment, security and so on. Effective agents deserve to be well paid for their services. It is impossible to say precisely at what point a company should know that it is moving towards getting involved in the payment of a bribe, but indicators are when:

- the representative claims close familiarity with the decision-maker in the contract concerned;
- the representative claims that he can arrange for the terms of the contract to be modified in the company's favour;
- it becomes evident that the representative is not taking his instructions from the company but from another person;
- the fee or commission being asked for is not commensurate with the work required from the representative;
- the representative stipulates that his commission must be paid offshore and that a disproportionate part must be paid on signing of the contract, not pro-rata to payments received by the seller.

In practice, a company should be able to recognise at an early stage whether it is dealing with a legitimate commercial agent or with the agent of a corrupt decision-maker. The sums of commission involved are never small. On a large and simple contract they could possibly be as low as 5%, but 10–15% is common and 25% is not unknown.

An alternative to the representative's commission, which is popular in some countries despite its extra complexity, is the nominal joint venture. A local company enters into partnership with the offshore contractor and receives a share of the proceeds of the contract that is disproportionate to its inputs. Even though this may be a tempting proposition where a long-term relationship rather than a single contract is envisaged, the company should consider carefully whether the proposed joint venture is genuine and legitimate, or whether it is merely another vehicle for the payment of a bribe. It is unlikely to be proposed in a country with a weak currency or tight foreign exchange controls because the benefits to the local partner will arise locally and not offshore.

In some countries it is common practice for a decision-making minister to request a contribution to the funds of the ruling party. Setting aside the question of whether there is any distinction between the party's funds and the minister's pocket, a political donation will be seen as a method of buying favourable treatment. This can reasonably be distinguished from a donation to a public project, such as a hospital or a university, which, if openly made and properly monitored, cannot be considered to be corrupt.

The damage

If it is assumed that the payer of a bribe will endeavour to recover the money in some way, then the cost of things further down the supply chain will be higher than they would otherwise be.

In countries suffering from a shortage of hard currency, harm is also caused by the fact that grand corruption bribes are almost always paid offshore. It is impossible to put a figure on how much goes offshore, but some years ago a Swiss source estimated that deposits held on behalf of African leaders in Swiss banks alone amounted to more than $20 billion, a sum that probably exceeded the total offshore indebtedness of the countries concerned. Consider the arms trade: between 1988 and 1994 the top ten arms-exporting countries sold an annual average of $30 billion-worth of weaponry, of which two-thirds went to developing countries. Industry insiders have estimated that not less than 15% of this value was effectively paid to decision-makers: politicians and military chiefs. Even if the figure was only 10%, $3 billion would have been diverted into the bank accounts of these individuals.

More important than the direct "cost" of grand corruption is the way that it distorts the decision-making process. Procurement policy is driven by personal gain rather than by the aims of usefulness, quality and cost, and may result in construction projects that are a poor use of scarce resources, or the purchase of equipment or goods that are unsuitable or of inferior quality. The national interest may be completely ignored in favour of projects or purchases whose only attraction is that they carry the potential for huge "commissions".

There is a tendency among businessmen in industrialised countries to consider grand corruption solely in economic terms. In developing countries, it is rightly seen as a moral issue as well, with one small group enriching themselves at the expense of their fellow countrymen and showing the way to those lower in the hierarchy whose petty corruption damages the whole framework of society.

No one should be in any doubt that companies that are parties to grand corruption, directly or indirectly, are doing serious harm to the country they are doing business with. In the short term, a contract may be won that otherwise would have been lost, but each act of corruption contributes to a further degrading of the business environment in which companies have to operate. It also carries the risk that the corruption will become public knowledge and therefore damaging to the company involved.

The weapons that can be used against it

The most important of the armoury of weapons that can be deployed against grand corruption is legislation that adequately addresses the issue. Until recently, the United States was the only country that could reasonably claim to have this. Under the 1977 Foreign Corrupt Practices Act (FCPA) it became as criminal for an American citizen to bribe a foreign public official as to bribe an official in the United States, although an exception was made for small "facilitation payments". Penalties include personal fines and prison sentences, as well as large corporate fines. There have not been many prosecutions under the FCPA, and its critics argue that this indicates that it has been ineffective. However, those who may be in the best position to judge, legal advisers to the largest corporations, appear to have no doubt that it has substantially improved the behaviour of corporate America.

The position outside the United States has changed significantly with the ratification, in February 1999, of the OECD Convention against the Bribery of Foreign Public Officials in International Business Transactions. Article 1 of the Convention reads as follows:

> Each Party shall take such measures as may be necessary to establish that it is a criminal offence under its law for any person intentionally to offer, promise or give any undue pecuniary or other advantage, whether directly or through intermediaries, to a foreign public official, for that official or for a third party, in order that the official act or refrain from acting in relation to the performance of official duties, in order to obtain or retain business or other improper advantage in the conduct of international business.

It is clear that the signatories to the convention, currently 34 of the world's major trading nations, have committed themselves to criminalising the bribery of foreign public officials (a broad definition including national and local politicians as well as national and local government employees). What is less clear is how easy it will be to enforce the convention. It is, for example, considered doubtful that a prosecution in the UK, based as it would currently have to be on the Corruption Act 1906, would have any chance of success; but the law governing corruption has been reviewed by the Law Commission and new legislation is expected. Meanwhile, other international groupings, including the Council of Europe, the European Union and the

Organisation of American States, are moving in the same direction as the OECD.

Criminalisation of offshore bribery would seem to place additional responsibilities on companies' external auditors, although the courts have yet to confirm that it does. Before the ratification of the OECD Convention, there was no reason for auditors who suspected that an offshore payment was a bribe to do anything more than satisfy themselves that it had been properly authorised within the company. A criminal payment cannot, of course, be properly authorised.

Similarly, offshore bribes have been tax deductible as legitimate business expenses. The British government has committed itself, independently of the OECD Convention, to ending this anomaly but has not yet done so. The intention is to shift the onus on to companies to prove that an offshore payment was not a bribe, rather than vice versa.

Many companies have established voluntary codes of conduct (or adopted the International Chamber of Commerce's recently revised code), which bans any form of corruption by company employees. The value and effectiveness of such codes depends to a great extent on the attitude toward them demonstrated by senior staff in the company. In some cases, it is required that they are re-signed annually to confirm that they have been complied with throughout the year. At worst, even if they are allowed to gather dust on a forgotten shelf, they can provide a measure of protection to "whistleblowers" who are unable to accept what some of their colleagues are doing and express their opinions publicly.

A system of competitive tendering for all substantial contracts and purchases is regarded by many as a strong defence against corruption. But in practice there are many ways in which a purchaser, if it is made worthwhile, can help a bidder win the contract. Some of these are as follows.

- Slanting the tender specification so that it favours one supplier.
- Holding a pre-qualifying competition, leading to a shortlist, which can eliminate potential threats to the favoured bidder.
- Agreeing to variations in the specification that assist the favoured bidder.
- Giving extra weight to intangible, non-price factors, such as "greater experience" or "better local representation", in the adjudicating of the bids.
- Agreeing privately with the favoured bidder that the scope of the contract will be substantially increased after it has been awarded, enabling them to submit a lower initial bid.

One example of how the tendering process can be converted was in a central African country where several international bidders were tendering to build a 30km section of highway. The minister of works called in the local representative, whom he knew well, of one of the companies and assured him that there would be a follow-on contract for a further 20km which would be awarded, without tender, to the winner of the first contract "at a price to be agreed". Thus the favoured company was able to cut its tender price drastically, in the certain knowledge that a further contract at highly profitable rates would be available.

Competitive tendering certainly makes life more complicated for the payers and receivers of corrupt payments than simple "negotiation". However, it cannot be relied upon to defeat them, unless the whole process, from initial specification to final implementation, is supervised by an individual or a body which does not stand to gain from a corrupt award.

This is where international institutions such as the World Bank are playing an increasingly significant role as they step up the measures they take to ensure that the funds they are providing to countries are not used for purposes other than those for which they were granted. This involves not only seeing that the projects and purchases they are co-financing are, in fact, of real national priority, but also ensuring that competitive bidding is genuinely competitive and not merely a cover for channelling business to a predetermined corrupt seller.

The risks for companies

As attitudes towards and legislation against corruption harden, the risk to companies that engage in it becomes more real and serious. Before the ratification of the OECD Convention, the risk to a non-American company was extremely low. The payment of the bribe was, of course, a criminal act in the country of the recipient. But as this person would usually be a member of the ruling regime, it would be unlikely that any action would follow even if the facts became widely known. The paying company could always fall back on the argument that by paying a "commission" it was only following local practice and could thereby emerge with its public image more or less intact. Perhaps the biggest risk was that a change of regime might scupper the deal after the bribe had been paid. This happened when the Shah of Iran was displaced in 1979 and the new government of Ayatollah Khomeini cancelled several contracts on which large "commissions" had already been paid.

Corruption may still be rife in some parts of the world, but the attitude to it has changed markedly. Less than a decade ago, in a BBC programme in 1994, Lord Young, previously secretary for trade and industry and, at the time of the broadcast, chairman of Cable & Wireless, said:

> Now when you're talking about kick-backs, you're talking about something that's illegal in this country and that, of course, you wouldn't dream of doing. I haven't even heard of one case in all my business life of anybody in this country doing things like that. But there are parts of the world I've been to where we all know that it happens. For example, I went to a Middle East country back in the 1970s and the first thing I saw was a legal agreement, drawn up by an English firm of solicitors, in which a relation of the ruler got a percentage off the top of every government contract. Now that is the accepted standard practice in that particular country. It is very different from our practice and would be totally wrong in our environment but wasn't wrong in their environment; and what we must be very careful of is not to insist that our practices are followed everywhere in the world.

Lord Young's principle of "When in Rome" is one that few would subscribe to today, let alone own up to. Companies are increasingly taking the view that the risks of suffering damage as a result of a corrupt act are greater than the benefits accruing from the act. Even if this is not the case now, when the OECD convention is given teeth and begins to bite it will undoubtedly become so.

Even now, companies that engage in corruption run the risk of being blacklisted by institutions which fund projects in less-developed countries. The World Bank has made it clear that it will not hesitate to debar, temporarily or permanently, any company it believes to have used corrupt means to win a contract in which the Bank is involved. One of the first substantial companies to be permanently debarred, in June 1999, from taking part in World Bank-financed contracts, was Case Technology of Watford, UK. It went into liquidation in December 1999.

Companies that are prepared to engage in corruption give out signals to their employees that it is all part of the game of business. And because money paid out in bribes has to be accounted for in opaque ways, someone with the authority to arrange payment of a bribe may at the same time decide to arrange the payment of an additional amount into an offshore bank account of their own. Such "reflux" is hard to identify, hard to control and another risk that corrupt companies face.

Petty corruption

A businessman visiting a developing country is travelling from the airport in the company car that has been sent to meet him. Suddenly the car is flagged down by two policemen, who say that it was exceeding the speed limit. The driver steps behind the car for a moment and then returns to his seat. "Are they charging you?" asks the visitor. "No, sir. They say $10 now or a $100 in court next week, so of course I pay." The visitor reimburses the driver.

This example demonstrates that although it should not be difficult for a company – and those who work for it – to appreciate why it should shun grand corruption, it may be much harder to take a stand against the making of small payments to public officials when these can speed up or unblock the bureaucratic process in procedures such as customs clearance. The amounts involved may seem too small to be bothered about, and why should you make your employees' lives more difficult by refusing to engage in what is common practice? But if it is alright to pay a public official something simply for doing his job, is it then acceptable to pay a larger sum to avoid the payment of customs duty or to ignore the fact that the goods being imported are prohibited? Where do you draw the line? All these acts are illegal.

Many expatriates will take the view that a small bribe is a victimless crime: wrong in principle but the sort of thing that is always going to happen in the real world. But they should ask themselves whether such a payment is:

- enabling them to jump the queue to the disadvantage of others;
- encouraging the disregard of the local law;
- helping to perpetuate a bureaucratic system that is corrupt and inefficient.

Petty corruption that permeates the system usually hits the most vulnerable members of society hardest. Some examples are:

- parents who cannot afford to pay the head teacher to admit a child to a "free" school place, or pay the doctor for "free" drugs or a hospital bed for a sick child;

- job-seekers who cannot get employment without paying a "fee" to the official in charge of hiring;
- shanty-dwellers who face eviction unless they make regular payments to the local policeman.

The list is endless. But although the payment of a bribe condones and encourages a practice that undermines the society in which it takes place, there are occasions when there really is no choice. This is illustrated by the experience of two people going to an anti-corruption conference in a small West African republic. On arrival they were told that they should have had vaccination certificates. Despite their protestations that smallpox has been eliminated, they were ushered in to see a doctor in a grubby white coat with an even grubbier syringe in front of him. They were told the cost of the vaccination was $20 and $40 was produced with alacrity. The syringe was left untouched and two vaccination certificates were issued. It made a good story at the conference.

Entertainment and small gifts
"There is no such thing as a free lunch" is often quoted. It highlights the tricky question of when entertainment and gifts become issues of petty corruption. Many companies have clear rules. At one extreme these may be unrealistically simple: "No gifts whatever may be given or received by company staff in connection with their work." This can cause embarrassment when a senior manager has to return a diary given by a valued supplier.

Four criteria can be used in determining the propriety of any gift: frequency, timing, reciprocity and value. In general, gifts should not be given more than once a year, typically at Christmas or at the time of a national festival. There should be extra sensitivity, however, if this coincides with the period of bidding for a major contract. There is a fundamental difference between a gift (even a modest one) given in the hope of winning a contract and a small gift in appreciation of having won a contract. The situation is, of course, eased if the other party gives hospitality or a small present in return. But much the most important consideration is the value of the gift, which should not, in any circumstance, represent more than a tiny fraction of the value of any business completed or under consideration.

Again, drawing the line can be difficult, as a UK-based multinational that won a competitive tender for a power station found. After the contract had been prepared, the foreign minister of energy said that he would prefer to sign it in London. The company agreed to pay his travel costs. The minister then said that he would like to bring his wife. The company decided that this was also acceptable. After arrival the minister's wife said that she wanted to go shopping but regretted that she did not have any money. At this point the company drew the line.

The most important consideration, however, must always be the openness with which any gift is given or received. The fact that the giving is done publicly, with no attempt at concealment, does not necessarily mean that it is beyond criticism. But if it is done surreptitiously, there will always be suspicion of corruption.

Conclusion

Corruption is not an easy issue. There will always be grey areas and borderline cases. But the following guidelines should be helpful.

- Grand corruption, in terms of the US Foreign Corrupt Practices Act and the OECD Convention, is always inexcusable, frequently (and increasingly often) criminal, and now carries grave risks for any company (or individual) that indulges in it.
- Petty corruption is also wrong and every effort should be made to avoid it. There are, however, circumstances in some countries in which it may be extremely difficult – or even dangerous – to do so. Without minimising its potential for damage, it is only realistic to recognise that individuals, particularly in isolation, may find themselves unable always to do the right thing.
- At times of doubt, "the newspaper test" is invaluable. If either the giver or the receiver of a present or a favour would be embarrassed to see the details accurately reported in a newspaper, there is a strong presumption of corruption.

In world terms, how important is corruption? James Wolfensohn, president of the World Bank, tells the story of how, on arrival to take up his new position, he was advised by more than one senior official that he should never mention "the C word". Since then, he has made a point of mentioning corruption in every speech that he makes.

10 Global sourcing

Keith Jones

WE'VE TRIED TO OPEN UP OUR PROCESSES BY ENGAGING WITH
STAKEHOLDERS ACROSS THE GLOBE; BY BEING THE FIRST COMPANY TO POST
ON THE INTERNET BOTH OUR FACTORY SITES AND THE RESULTS OF OUR
EXTERNAL AUDITS OF THOSE SITES. WARTS AND ALL.
Hannah Jones, European Director of Corporate Responsibility, Nike Inc.

ONE OF THE drivers of the globalisation of business has been the increase in global sourcing by companies in the developed world. Across all sectors, companies routinely buy goods from suppliers in India, China and other parts of Asia and are now extending their supply chains to the burgeoning economies of Eastern Europe. Global sourcing is a fact of business life, as competitive pressures will continue to force companies to source from wherever pricing is keenest for the required standards of quality.

Today's consumers are hungry for variety and choice, but they still want to pay as little as possible. Low prices, however, often reflect low wages and poor working conditions along the supply chain. Factories in the special economic zones of south China are being undercut by Vietnamese suppliers, who in turn are looking over their shoulders at Mongolia, where prices are even lower.

Not so long ago, Western companies could ignore the link between low supplier prices and poor employment conditions. Cost cutting has been a cornerstone of many corporate strategies and finding cheaper suppliers is an obvious way of reducing costs. It used to be common for global companies to be ignorant of both the geographical location and the identity of their suppliers. Today, such ignorance is not bliss. The consumer demanding low prices is also beginning to think and care about working conditions along a company's supply chain. This is largely because of the increase in pressure groups that draw attention to what they see as unacceptable exploitation. Pressure-group activity and whistle-blowing have become meat and drink to the media and have resulted in damaging publicity for a number of well-known firms such as Nike, the Gap and Next.

Not all the ethical problems of procurement are in Asia: many arise in the former Soviet bloc. For example, a factory in the former Soviet republic of Latvia, which used to employ over 13,000 people, currently employs fewer than 3,000, mainly women, making garments for women. It has adapted to a market environment and is profitable. But it has achieved this by making its staff work seven days a week with compulsory overtime. For Marks and Spencer, one of its British customers, this poses a problem. Having been the subject of criticism for treating its British suppliers badly, M&S does not want to be further accused of exploiting workers overseas.

Such dilemmas will become common and will force procuring companies to take steps to rectify glaring anomalies in working conditions along the supply chain. They may be helped in this by political change in that Eastern European countries that join the European Union will enter a world of greater regulation and control, extending into the area of social accountability. This will require them to make big changes in their employment and labour practices, although they will get financial help from the EU to do this.

Western companies are finding themselves exposed on ethical issues as never before. They face the danger of appearing complacent at best and exploitative at worst, as pressure groups and the media confront them with evidence of unpalatable practices among their suppliers. The list could include:

- child and family labour;
- extended hours of work;
- poor safety standards and enforcement;
- routinely discriminatory practices;
- management styles that appear harsh compared with Western standards.

Protecting the integrity of the brand

In an ethically conscious environment, companies that refuse to accept any responsibility for the practices of their suppliers run the risk of damaging their brand and thereby undermining the value of their business. In the global marketplace, the biggest threat to brand strength (and hence brand value) is an attack on a brand's ethical integrity. In an age of immediate mass communication, a camcorder pointed judiciously in a factory the other side of the world can have a devastating impact on a brand's reputation. Good brands are high-value assets and any risks they may face need to be anticipated and guarded against.

General Motors, for example, was exposed by consumer rights activists for producing cars that were inherently unsafe; Shell was accused of exploiting a rural community in Nigeria; and Nike was shown to be producing trainers in sub-standard conditions. These three companies are now pioneers in the area of social and ethical accountability and have implemented effective social and ethical monitoring systems that are thoroughly integrated into their business operations. Their experiences reveal that in a changing global environment, the ethical management of supply chains is not an optional extra but an integral part of brand management.

The importance attributed to brand value means that companies are likely to come under increasing pressure to demonstrate that their supply-chain management supports and reinforces the values and behaviours espoused by their brand. Asserting that they are will not be sufficient. Instead, firms will need to demonstrate that they are investing in the development of social and ethical programmes along the supply chain, and that these are being monitored by independent specialists. Thus brand value will be increased because the ethical component is publicly and independently demonstrated.

After the exposure mentioned above, Nike's brand value declined sharply, a fact which most commentators attributed to the internet-based negative publicity the brand was getting. The challenge to companies in such a position is to secure improvements in the supply chain. Social responsibility programmes and their audit are not cheap, but their cost should be seen against the financial hit that, for example, a negative publicity programme could have on a firm's sales or share price.

Tangible financial benefits often take time to filter to the bottom line, as Grupo M, a supplier of Levi Strauss, discovered. Based in the Dominican Republic, the company has made significant financial investments in a range of initiatives enabling it to comply with Levi Strauss's "terms of engagement" for suppliers. Grupo M has now introduced further employment benefits, including day-care centres and medical and dental services, because they have proven their ability to generate significant bottom-line benefits. The company now enjoys very low rates of absenteeism and no strikes. It is able to meet quality standards that have enabled it to win contracts from a number of leading retailers, including Marks and Spencer, Polo and Liz Claiborne.

A crucial component of any improvement programme is the involvement of non-governmental organisations (NGOs). The burgeoning world of NGOs now encompasses trade unions, as well as charities such as Oxfam and independent support organisations, often co-operatively run. These organisations have a valuable role to play in changing a supplier's operations. They act as independent advocates and specialist advisers. Their moral authority and influence, like their access to the media, is considerable, both with government and the public.

For example, if a company wants a textile supplier to stop relying on child labour, it must consider the scale of the impact on the incomes of local families. Any joint improvement programme between the procuring company and its suppliers would need to explore whether other family members could be employed to help replace a child's lost income. NGOs can play a vital role in helping to identify and resolve such issues in supply-chain management and in driving what is known as "remediation" activity.

The following section outlines the steps that companies can take to create a social accountability programme, starting from the basics of implementing policies and gathering data, through to developing a partnership with suppliers based on shared ethical values and a sustained programme of continuous improvement.

Credibility through accountability

At the heart of ethical procurement management is accountability: a willingness among both corporate leaders and their employees to supply an "account" of the company's operations and activities to society at large. Companies can initiate this dialogue by taking the following steps.

Accountability through gathering data

The first step is obtaining data about the suppliers themselves. A surprising number of companies do not even know who all their suppliers actually are or where they are located. Much of the contractual and technical information for a comprehensive database on the corporate supply chain will come from the purchaser's own records, as well as from employees at head office and field operations. However, much of the detailed operational information must come from suppliers themselves. Companies often gather such information through self-assessment questionnaires circulated to their suppliers.

The weakness inherent in self-assessment is self-evident. A supplier company is unlikely to admit to child labour, for example, or paying inadequate wages, or offering unsafe conditions. But the way questions are framed can make a difference. For example, asking how many people are employed in various age groups (over 65, 30–65, 16–30, under 16) is more likely to reveal the incidence of child labour than the straightforward: "How many children under 16 do you employ?" A self-assessment evaluation that is introduced sensitively and backed up by a full communications programme is more likely to obtain the supplier's commitment and create an effective platform for further improvements. Even if supplier information proves to be invalid, as it often does, a framework for any subsequent independent audit will at least have been established.

Ethical codes of conduct

The next step is to make a public statement of the company's commitment to a given set of ethical values. Such a code should be viewed as a set of rules against which the company is willing to be judged. The code should go far beyond the unsupported statements and claims of being an "ethical company" that so many blue-chip companies still include in their annual reports.

Codes of conduct are now widespread and they are all different, with some firms accepting, for example, use of child labour in limited, controlled circumstances.

External codes of conduct

These are aimed at improving industry-wide standards, and are often created through partnerships between businesses, NGOs and stakeholders. Typically, such codes basically outlaw child labour, forced labour and discrimination, and require adequate wages and controlled hours as well as safe conditions.

Examples include a code of conduct promoted by the World Federation of Sporting Goods Industry (WFSGI), an organisation made up of companies seeking to improve best practice across the sporting goods industry (www.wfsgi.org). The Fair Labour Association (FLA), an American-based non-profit organisation, has championed a similar initiative in an attempt to protect the rights of apparel and footwear workers throughout the world (www.Ichr.org). It is largely made up of human rights, labour rights and consumer organisations, but ten companies, including Adidas-Solomon, Reebok and Phillips Van Heusen, have also agreed to comply with FLA standards.

In the UK, the Ethical Trading Initiative (ETI) is an alliance between retail or consumer goods companies, NGOs and trade unions with the aim of improving labour conditions along global supply chains. The British government's Department for International Development has given the ETI financial and political support. ETI membership requires companies to comply with the requirements of its so-called Base Code. The framework sets various standards in areas such as collective bargaining, child labour, working hours and regularity of employment. Sainsbury's, a British supermarket group, has used the code to target a number of its suppliers, including wine makers in South Africa and banana growers in Costa Rica.

Many companies follow these industry-based codes as an alternative or as a supplement to their own ethical codes of conduct. However, these fast-multiplying codes have a number of potential drawbacks.

- The variations in company ethical codes can result in audit outcomes being unclear and inconclusive.
- There is no requirement for enforcement unless companies use independent verification for the implementation of their codes.
- Supplier factories may be audited many times by different clients with different codes.

The International Ethical Standard: SA8000

A big step forward in ethics management has been the development of SA8000, an international social accountability standard to evaluate whether companies and other organisations are complying with basic standards of labour and human rights practices. It developed from the growing recognition that global supply chains can and should be subject to an independent objective assessment. An independent audit helps to improve the ethical standards of the supply chain and demonstrates to the outside world that companies are taking steps to ensure that their supply chains have appropriate standards.

The SA8000 standard is based on International Labour Organisation (ILO) conventions on issues such as forced labour and freedom of association, as well as the Universal Declaration of Human Rights and the United Nations Convention on the Rights of the Child. For example, on child labour, which it defines as children aged 15 years or less, it says:

- The company shall not engage in or support exploitative child labour.
- The company shall establish, document, maintain, and effectively communicate policies and procedures, where appropriate, for promotion of education for non-displaced children who are either subject to the local compulsory education laws or are leaving school, including means to ensure:

- that no such worker is employed during regular school hours;
- that their combined hours of daily work time, school-time and transportation time to and from either activity does not exceed eight hours a day;
- that, in relevant work activities, no work shall be permitted for such workers during those time periods during the day that are unhealthy, unsafe, or hazardous to children, inclusive of transportation.

Compliance with the requirements of SA8000 produces independent certification: credible and visible evidence that an organisation is meeting internationally agreed social accountability standards. Social Accountability International (SAI), founded in 1997 as the Council on Economic Priorities Accreditation Agency (CEPAA), is the accreditation agency and a number of certification bodies have gained accreditation. The first was SGS–ICS (International Certification Services) in the United States, closely followed by BVQI (Bureau Veritas Quality International) in the UK, DNV (Det Norske Veritas) in Hong Kong and ITS (Intertek Testing Service) in the United States. These auditing agencies issue the SA8000 certificates once they are satisfied that companies have complied with the requirements of the standard.

Hundreds of social accountability audits have been carried out by these specialist certification bodies throughout the world on behalf of European and American companies. Their experience reveals that social accountability auditing is often complex, mainly because of the range and number of stakeholders (employees, managers and representatives of local communities) that are interviewed in focus groups.

The audit measures processes and practices in the context of local norms and standards. For instance, because many employees in Asia live in factory accommodation, auditors pay particular attention to the condition of dormitory accommodation and related issues of segregation and overcrowding. However, because it is the accepted standard in, say, China and other countries, the auditors may decide that a hardboard sheet on a metal-frame bunk bed in a room with six or eight other people is acceptable. Toilet facilities have to meet basic requirements of privacy, segregation and cleanliness, but in all other respects will be assessed according to regional standards, not the standards found in, say, London or New York.

The auditors' relationships with their focus-group participants can be especially difficult. Issues of communications across cultures and languages dominate. Great care and effort has to be taken to ensure that the auditors obtain usable objective information, not merely a distorted personal account. Alternative information-gathering methods often have to be used to ensure the validity of the information acquired from focus groups.

A social accountability audit often throws up some peculiar on-site anomalies. In China, where there is a legal restriction of one child per family, additional children may be born and concealed within the extended family. It is not uncommon for such young people to replace their "legitimate" siblings in factories, thereby producing a disparity between the observed and the "official" age of a worker.

If an audited company is judged to be failing to conform to international standards, the auditors make various recommendations for improvement. The audited company can adopt these measures as part of a process of improvement and then resubmit itself for SA8000. Underpinning this approach is a widespread belief that SA8000 should be used to encourage and support non-compliant suppliers, rather than castigate them or cause them to lose crucial business contracts. Ostracising these suppliers would only harm the very people that the international community is seeking to help: the already disadvantaged workers. Improvement, not disqualification, is the preferred outcome.

The birth of SA8000 was controversial. Some organisations feared that it would put too much emphasis on the interests of business and would fail to pay enough attention to wider interest groups such as NGOs and community groups. Others feared that the proposed standard would distract from issues such as environmental control.

In practice, these fears have proved unfounded. SA8000 is proving to be a robust and flexible tool of ethical management practice and its criteria can be used by firms that do not yet reach its standards to raise their game. Management teams can, for example, use the standard to conduct their own supply-chain audit and thereby identify the improvements and controls necessary for them to qualify for SA8000.

Supplier partnership programmes

The success of any supply-chain audit programme depends on the extent of co-operation and trust between procuring companies and their suppliers. Such partnerships take time and effort to establish since they require companies with operations involving different working practices and different languages, cultures and values to commit to a shared set of ethical goals.

Promoting ethical codes among suppliers

Acceptance and ownership of the values and principles of a company code is important. One company's letter to its suppliers is typical, although some may find the tone patronising.

May I, on behalf of the board of directors of our company, extend a warm personal welcome to you on becoming part of the global partnership of our supplier network.

With this letter, I am attaching our Aspirational Statement, which I hope you will take time to study carefully, and seek to implement. This represents our aspirations for all our suppliers in the area of human rights and the environment and is the ethical framework within which we intend to conduct all our business.

We recognise that not all of the Statement can be achieved immediately, but we are pledged to support any of our suppliers who is genuinely trying to implement improvements and striving to meet our aspirations.

I look forward to strengthening and extending our business and ethical partnership with you in the coming years.

Supply-chain partnerships also require substantial investment from procuring companies. To achieve these ethical goals and gain real improvements along the supply chain, procuring companies must help their suppliers introduce and sustain a regimen of continuous improvement – introducing, for example, full fume extraction, or progressively reducing overtime hours worked by recruiting more staff. This is probably the most effective management strategy for safeguarding company values against supply-chain social accountability failures.

Effective partnerships have to be built and maintained, they do not just happen. Research by business schools, such as that at Sheffield University, shows that the way relationships between individuals are handled, both externally and internally, is crucial. Codes and guidelines will achieve a certain amount. But a great deal can be achieved if they are combined with personal support and creative approaches, continual monitoring and genuine engagement.

Sustaining supplier partnerships is a challenge even for sophisticated global companies. The difficulties and complexities of such relationship management are often underestimated or even ignored. Functional barriers should be disregarded in favour of a cross-departmental attitude of co-operation that allows for sensible decisions to be made. Senior management plays a critical role in sustaining everyone's commitment by demonstrating board-level enthusiasm for social accountability goals and initiatives.

Conclusion

In a world of increasing price competition, companies are under ever-greater pressure to squeeze savings from their global supply chains. The increasing number of discerning customers and strident lobby groups is a strong counter pressure. Corporate leaders have the unenviable task of trying to resolve these opposing forces. At some stage, they must decide whether their operations should be ethically and socially accountable. If they take this step, they must accept that ethical management is a viable activity that can help drive decisions about global sourcing strategy and the nature of supplier relationships. Moreover, the experiences of a few pioneering companies suggests that ethical global sourcing has the potential to become a dynamic force, leading to many improvements and innovations in products and processes along global supply chains.

Companies that decide to take the social accountability route can take a number of practical steps to transform the way they do business with overseas suppliers. The best safeguard against unwelcome accusations of exploitation along the supply chain is for companies to:

- establish codes of conduct;
- outline and explain their vision of ethical global sourcing;
- gather better data about their suppliers; and
- introduce comprehensive audit programmes along the supply chain conducted by independent auditors.

Companies need to consider tapping into the experience of independent inspection bodies as it is the most secure method of conducting supplier audits. Inspection organisations offer extensive experience in the social and ethical accountability area and their certification now has international recognition and status.

As they become more experienced in ethically based procurement, companies should aim to develop close partnerships with their suppliers. They need to become adept at relationship management to ensure these partnerships are effective, otherwise edicts from company clients will be simply evaded or ignored by over-committed factory owners desperate to shave a lower price to remain competitive. In the best supplier relationships, such close arrangements are already in place, but, in the future, they will have to become the norm rather than the honourable exception.

These types of embedded supplier partnerships that promote continual improvement are fast becoming the basis of successful risk management in sourcing strategy. Companies that choose to remain ignorant about the practices of their suppliers do so at their peril.

4

BEYOND RULES AND REGULATIONS

11 Values-based codes

Simon Webley

A CODE OF ETHICS UNDERPINS THE VALUES OF ANY BUSINESS. WITHOUT IT, A CORPORATION WILL HAVE NO MORAL COMPASS.

      Kenneth Rushton, Director, Institute of Business Ethics, London

MANY LARGE CORPORATIONS set out their purposes and values as part of the job of managing stakeholder relationships. But if these laudable statements are to have any real effect, companies must translate them into practical guidelines for their employees and others with whom they do business. Such guidelines, or ethical codes, set out desirable conduct and best practice, and provide frameworks to help employees resolve ethical dilemmas they may encounter in their work.

As Chapter 2 indicates, there has been a significant increase in the use of ethical codes of conduct by American and British companies. This chapter provides practical guidance about how to develop and implement such codes, in both a national and an international context.

Ethical codes typically spell out a company's obligations to five constituencies.

- Employees
- Shareholders and other contributors of finance
- Suppliers
- Customers
- The community (including its physical environment)

There are others with whom a company has dealings, such as their competitors and national governments, but most codes using a stakeholder model focus on five sets of relationships.

Although most codes share this common framework, no two codes look the same; there is no such thing as a model code. An effective and credible code is one that reflects the concerns of employees and others at different levels and locations in an organisation. It should be alive in the sense of constantly evolving and responding to emerging issues in business. For instance, many recently created or revised codes tackle real 21st-century problems, such as software copying, substance abuse, the use of the Internet by employees and workplace harassment.

Setting the structure

An organisation wishing to develop and implement a code of business ethics should find the following template useful.

INTRODUCTION

Usually signed by the chairman or chief executive, or both, this starts with a sentence on the purpose of the code, mentioning the values, such as integrity, responsibility and reputation, that are important in the conduct of the business. It describes the commitment of the organisation and those who lead it to maintaining high standards both internally and externally in order to enhance its reputation and thus the long-term sustainability of the business.

PURPOSE

What the business is about: the products it makes or services it provides, its financial objectives and its role in society.

EMPLOYEES

The company's policies on such matters as working conditions, recruitment, training and development, rewards, health and safety, equal opportunities, retirement, redundancy, discrimination and harassment, and the use of company assets by employees.

CUSTOMERS

The company's attitude to its customers with regard to, for example, business terms, quality, pricing, information, after-sales service and customer satisfaction.

SHAREHOLDERS AND FINANCE PROVIDERS

The company's attitude to those who fund it with regard to, for example, the return they can expect, the protection of their investment, and the information provided to them about the company's achievements and prospects.

SUPPLIERS

The company's attitude to its suppliers, including payment terms, co-operative efforts aimed at, say, improving quality and efficiency, and rules governing gifts and hospitality.

THE COMMUNITY

This may emphasise the spirit as well as the letter of the law and will cover such things as the company's environmental policy, its involvement in local affairs and its policy on supporting charities.

Getting going

The initiative to produce a code usually comes from someone high up in the organisation. To get off the ground and succeed it must be supported by the chairman and chief executive. Existing policies – for example, on bribery, discrimination or use of company property for personal use – will be useful starting points for constructing the code.

In order to ensure that the code addresses real issues and current concerns, companies should consult employees at all levels in a carefully structured way. In general, the more people are involved, the greater the sense of commitment there will be among employees, provided their views are genuinely taken into account and pertinent issues are not overlooked or fudged.

Presentation

It is best for one person to be responsible for drafting the code. Once it is tested, tuned and agreed it must be endorsed and issued by the board of directors. The process for implementation must also be agreed – decisions about its use are as important as the decision to have a code.

The support of senior staff should be secured as early as possible. Early involvement of the legal, human resources and public affairs functions is also crucial. Taking time to explain the meaning and principles of the code will make the difference between having something that actually makes a difference or is ignored.

Employees

The success of a code hinges on whether employees perceive it as important and relevant. Decisions on how the code should be positioned and promoted to employees are therefore critical. At a minimum, each employee should receive a personal copy; merely posting it on notice-boards will have little effect. A more active step is to link the code to employment policies or even performance appraisals. For example, many firms make their code an integral part of their employees' contracts. Those that do generally find that the code is better known and followed.

Employees are unlikely to grasp the full meaning and implications of the code or their obligation to uphold it, unless it is explained to them personally. For new employees, it should be included in the joining instructions or induction training and staff manuals. This should be followed up by regular reference to the code in training programmes.

Many companies find that it is hard to sustain interest in the code and ensure that it percolates through the company's culture. So a continuous awareness programme is required. The inclusion of ethical dilemmas (perhaps in the form of a short case study) in company training programmes has proved effective in helping overcome ethical apathy.

External use

External knowledge that a company has a code of ethics is good for its reputation. Copies of the code should be made available to shareholders, partners, recruitment agencies, suppliers and other organisations with which the company has dealings.

Customers are also entitled to know how the company does business. Some firms provide "consumer charters" or codes with their products, or print them on the back of invoices or receipts. Such public statements are an open invitation to people to measure a company's performance according to the standards it espouses. It can be risky but those who set out their position usually find it can be a means of sustaining customer and employee loyalty.

Suppliers must also be given details of any relevant parts of a code in order to shape expectations and avoid misunderstandings. Some companies ask suppliers to report possible breaches of the code that they notice in the course of doing business with the company. If a company is committed to taking action on any reported ethical failures, the code can help to build trust with suppliers.

Public pressure for high standards has led to companies being asked to ensure that suppliers, especially but not exclusively in developing countries, observe minimum requirements for health and safety, and the employment of children.

Implementing a code

The accepted best practice is for a small group of senior staff, often with a non-executive director as chairman, to be given responsibility to implement the code and to monitor its adoption and effectiveness. Such a body should:

- see that systems are established that will encourage, even enforce, compliance with the code;

- see that training is provided for how the code is to be applied;
- investigate alleged breaches of the code;
- regularly review the code's wording and content in the light of new ethical issues.

The monitoring of the use or abuse of an ethics programme, including the code, is usually delegated to a senior departmental head. The company secretary or general counsel is the function most commonly selected but corporate affairs, internal audit and compliance are not uncommon. In the United States, it is now normal to find a designated ethics officer in both head office and other locations where the company operates. The main function of those in charge of ethics programmes is providing advice, investigating apparent breaches of codes, training in resolving ethical dilemmas and ensuring that managers are operating their departments in accordance to the standards set out in the company's codes. Many operate confidential helplines which can be used either to alert senior management to some dubious practice or simply to ask for help in understanding how to handle an ethical issue. Some companies prefer to outsource their confidential helpline facility. This is largely because it gives credibility to the confidentiality aspect of the policy.

Some consideration should be given to show how a code is applied and monitored at company locations in different countries. Certainly the core values of a company should never be compromised but local applications of clauses in a code will need discussion with local managers. Furthermore, there may be local ethical issues which are not covered by the code of conduct issued in the headquarter country. These need to be addressed in local versions of the company's code – which of course, should be in the local language.

There is a danger that monitoring procedures that concentrate on compliance will undermine the main purpose of codes – namely to set standards and give guidance. The overall purpose is to embed a culture of ethical sensitivity throughout the organisation.

Violation of a code

If an ethical code is to have any credibility, a company must be willing to discipline any employee found guilty of a breach of it. The procedure should be kept simple and should involve the legal officer of the company. The grounds of the accusation need to be given to the person involved and the company's disciplinary procedure carefully followed.

Reported cases of bribery in Shell

| | Numbers of bribes and total value $ | | | |
	1997	1998	1999	2000
Bribes offered and/or paid by Shell company employees directly or indirectly to third parties	0	1 ($300)	1 ($300)	0
Bribes offered and/or paid by intermediaries, contractor employees directly or indirectly to third parties	*	*	0†	1 ($4,562)
Bribes solicited and/or accepted by Shell company employees	23 (small)	4 ($75,000)	3 ($153,000)	4 ($89,000)
Bribes solicited and/or accepted by intermediaries, contractor employees or others	*	*	1 (unknown)	1 (zero)§

*Data not available.
†One case in which a Shell employee used an intermediary to make payments of US$300 has been included in the cases concerning company employees.
§Bribe refused and reported by Shell company employee.

This would normally involve the person suspected of unethical practice being supported by a person of their choice, such as a trade union representative. Depending on the seriousness of the case, the discipline would range from a warning to dismissal.

For example, Shell's 2001 annual report provides details of disciplinary action taken by the company against staff who have breached the company's code with regard to bribery (see above).

In the difficult situation of an employee being asked by a senior employee to act unethically, there should be some way for the case to be heard without prejudice to the junior person's position. This clearly requires sensitive handling. Normally an independent person – that is someone more senior than the alleged offender and from another department – should be asked by the company secretary to investigate the case. Where whistleblowing is involved, there will probably be credible evidence of malpractice in paper records. Where the problem is harassment, discrimination or bullying, interviews of a number of people will have to take place and identities will have to be protected.

The difficulty in these cases is to distinguish between grudge or revenge by a dissatisfied employee and genuine cases of breaches of the code. An open culture in the organisation and effective grievance procedures that are trusted by the staff can considerably reduce the number of potential whistleblowing cases.

Handling ethical dilemmas or disagreements

There will be situations that have not been anticipated by the code and where no clear consensus exists among employees about how to behave in the particular circumstances. For example, an individual employee may be faced with an unusually difficult moral choice (see Chapter 4).

In cases involving complex ethical questions, or where different ethics appear to collide, feelings among employees can run high, especially when managers follow a course of action that is felt to be unjust or immoral. Usually, these actions involve the treatment of individuals, though they can involve a wider group.

Managers must accept that controversial ethical issues will arise and plan how they will deal with them. Those responsible for implementing and overseeing the ethical code need to build in opportunities for debate and feedback about the working of the code. A lack of dialogue with employees is often at the root of internal disagreements about ethics.

Cross-cultural problems

The most difficult areas of business ethics concern dilemmas that arise when doing business in countries where laws, values and customs are different from those of the headquarters country. This applies not just to global companies but also to businesses that have investments in overseas countries or joint ventures, partnerships or trading relationships with foreign companies. In emerging markets, for example, there may be inadequate information, volatile and unstable financial regimes and close host-government involvement. Managers may find themselves caught up in difficult issues of right and wrong and may need to choose between the company's obligations to domestic stakeholders and its obligations to the host country.

In his book on the ethics of international business, Tom Donaldson highlights eight major issues that multinationals must address when "internationalising" their domestic codes of business practice.[1] These are:

- bribery and corrupt payments;
- employment and personnel issues;

- marketing practices;
- the impact of the multinational on the development of host countries;
- effects on the natural environment;
- cultural impacts of multinational operations;
- relations with host governments;
- relations with home countries.

If these issues are not addressed in guidelines drawn up with the involvement of local directors, problems will almost certainly emerge in at least one and possibly all of these areas. The aim must be to anticipate the problems before they become public issues. One example is the principle of the equal treatment of men and women. Most domestic codes of ethics have a policy on non-discrimination on grounds of gender; indeed, many say they have an equal opportunities policy. Yet in countries where a Muslim culture predominates, the policy has to be applied in a different way from that which is normal in a Judeo-Christian culture. For instance, Unilever's chairman discussed in a speech in 1997, how the principle of "equal opportunities" for everyone included in his company's code could be brought into line with a legal ban on women working outside the home. He stated:

> That ban is based on religious principles and is applied in, for instance, Saudi Arabia. We feel that we must respect the culture and the law of the land, regardless of our personal view on this. That means that no women work in our businesses there. For the men who work there the principle of 'equal opportunities' applies in full and nationality, social status or religious background are not allowed to play a role in recruitment or promotion.[2]

An analysis of the codes of ten multinationals[3] indicates that the most common cross-cultural issues addressed were:

- gifts (hospitality and bribes);
- conflicts of interest;
- insider dealing;
- equal opportunities and discrimination;
- protection of the environment.

These ten firms recommended approaches that were universally applicable. Furthermore, they communicated the policy to their employees and partners throughout the world. The codes were prefaced with strong statements from chairmen, presidents and CEOS explaining the importance of the document and clear guidance about how it was to be used.

For example, policies on the giving and receiving of gifts or favours and of paying facilitation payments are often controversial. Many companies and government departments or agencies do not allow this. However, in some cultures it is considered offensive not to accept or give modest gifts. Company policies differ. Some examples of polices contained in codes of ethics are as follows.

HONEYWELL

> *No employee will give, offer or promise to give, or ask for or accept anything of value ... with the following exceptions: items of a strictly advertising nature (that is, imprinted with the company's name ...) which are less than $10 in value.*

STANDARD CHARTERED BANK

> *Nothing may be given or received which might distort commercial judgement or harm the Group's reputation ... Any business-related personal benefit which you or your family give or receive must be reported in writing within three working days to the person to whom you normally report.*

BRITISH AIRWAYS

> *We must not accept gifts or hospitality of significant value from firms or individuals ... these are deemed business favours and by accepting them we might compromise our position.*

International guidelines

International bodies, such as the International Chamber of Commerce, have produced worldwide standards of practice on areas such as extortion and bribery, and advertising and marketing. Other useful documents are the *1999 OECD Guidelines on Multinational Corporations*, the *1998 ILO Declaration on Fundamental Principles on Rights at Work* and the principles on environment and sustainable development following the Rio (1992) and Kyoto (1997) summit meetings. These can help companies to draw up codes that reflect both best practice and internationally acknowledged standards.

Recent work in integrating international standards has focused on the thinking of Hans Kung and others under the general heading of "A global ethic for global business". Out of it has come the following.

- The UN Global Compact[4]
- The Caux Roundtable's Principles for Business[5]
- The Global Sullivan Principles[6]
- An Interfaith Declaration: A Code of Ethics on International Business[7]

All of the above address cross-cultural problems associated with establishing universal agreement on standards of business behaviour. For example, the UN *Declaration of Human Rights and the Principles on environmental sustainability*, set out in the ISO 14000 series of standards, is helping to create agreement about the content of a global ethic.

Human rights and environmental sustainability are two areas where it has proved possible to achieve a level of agreement. Trickier areas have included bribery, although the OECD Convention on this (see Chapter 9), represents a big step forward.

The important task for companies is to develop core values that can be applied locally and to make them widely known, not only among their staff but also among those with whom they do business. Global principles require local expression if they are to be of practical value.

Beyond the code

Ethical codes play an important role in creating ethically accountable businesses. They help to forge a valuable consensus on ethical behaviour in a world where people often rationalise their actions on the grounds of expediency or pragmatism. The "ethical sensitivity" of an individual may accommodate the payment of a bribe to secure an export order but be outraged by, say, the lies told by a colleague for the sake of personal advancement. A code of conduct or ethics clarifies where lines are drawn and discretion ends or is limited.

A senior manager in a company that has operated a code of ethics for many years speaks of the need for realistic expectations and willingness to compromise. He explains:

> *Ethical perfection is an unrealistic goal, not only because of the limitations inherent in the human condition, but because ethical goals often conflict, and the most difficult issues are those that require accommodations and compromise among competing ethical goals.*

Ultimately, it is individuals who will determine the ethical quality of business conduct. Personal integrity and commitment to high moral values begin in the family, are nurtured in schools and colleges and are matured at work. There, people will need to be reminded regularly of the need for individual and business integrity, which includes adherence to stated principles and codes but also requires a standard of conduct that extends beyond printed guidelines.

United Biscuits, in the introduction to its *Company's Statement on Ethics and Operating Principles*, puts it succinctly:

> *We believe in and obey both the letter and spirit of the law but the law is the minimum and no set of rules can provide all the answers or cover all questionable situations. While it is the responsibility of top management to keep a company honest and honourable, perpetuating ethical values is not a function only of the chief executive or a handful of senior managers. Every employee is expected to take on the responsibility of always behaving ethically, whatever the circumstances. Beliefs and values must always come before policies, practices and goals; the latter must be altered if they violate fundamental beliefs.*

12 Accounting for ethics

Mike Peirce

THE CASE FOR SOCIAL AND ENVIRONMENTAL AUDITS TO SUPPLEMENT THE
ANNUAL REPORT AND ACCOUNTS IS BEING ACCEPTED BY A SMALL BUT
GROWING NUMBER OF MULTINATIONALS. THERE IS NO MISTAKING THE
DIRECTION OF THE UNDERLYING TREND.

Will Hutton, Director of the Industrial Society

ELEVEN MEMBERS OF the UK Society of Motor Manufacturers and
Traders commit to an automotive sector strategy with targets on a
path towards sustainable development. Camelot, the UK's lottery
operator, produces a social report based on wide-ranging dialogue, using
an expert panel to champion the interests of stakeholders during the
audit process. The US apparel companies, Nike and the Gap join the
International Youth Foundation initiative, the Global Alliance, to
improve the work and life opportunities of young adult workers. The
corporate, trade union and NGO alliance – the Ethical Trading Initiative
– monitors labour standards in the supply of wine from South Africa,
horticultural products from Zimbabwe and clothing from China.
Southern Sun Group in South Africa commits to using accountability
principles as a guide to "systematically improving its social and ethical
accounting and reporting".

Many initiatives, many different sectors and countries, many different
reasons – the common thread being that these companies recognise the
importance of business behaviour and the role of business in society.
This recognition has led firms to introduce systems that:

- **manage and measure** social and environmental as well as
  economic performance;
- **integrate** ethical issues in decision-making processes;
- **communicate** to employees, shareholders and other external
  groups the values underlying their activities and their impact on
  society.

In part, the companies are responding to pressure from society.

- **More is known about business.** More information on organisations and the impact of their activities is publicly available at a low cost or free.
- **The role of business is changing.** As power has shifted away from government towards business, governments, international institutions and society are increasingly looking to business to help resolve such issues as social exclusion, poverty and environmental damage.
- **The accountability of business is widening.** Traditionally, businesses have been perceived as accountable to their shareholders, whereas today the interests of a wide variety of stakeholders are increasingly recognised and advocated by government, regulators and influential pressure groups.

At the same time, companies are beginning to see that their financial interests and their ethical concerns do not operate in separate spheres. As illustrated in Chapter 1, the growth of the knowledge company and the new-economy need for innovation in ways of partnering and learning have bound economics and people more closely together (see www.innovation-partnership.org).

Yet intentions do not translate easily into reality. Companies often find it difficult to ensure that their values and goals are reflected in the behaviour of their employees and the results of their activities. And even when companies have a clear sense of their goals, they operate in a complex environment in which strategic aspirations may be in conflict with the needs of some or all of their stakeholders. There may also be a lack of consensus between and within stakeholder groups about the desirability of different choices and different outcomes. So in this complex and contested environment, are there any right decisions? If there are, how does the company reach them, how does it put them into practice and how does it measure and communicate the results?

The social and ethical accounting process

It is in the context of increased stakeholder pressure on organisations and a heightened ambition to manage ethical as well as financial performance that the practice of social and ethical accounting, auditing and reporting has developed. The accounting process seeks to identify what it means for a particular company to be ethical as well as to understand and communicate performance on ethical issues. Acknowledging the variety in practice, this chapter outlines a generic model of social and ethical accounting, identifying key principles and aspects of the process and how different companies have adopted these. It then examines the role of standards and guidelines in the development of social and ethical accounting, and how the use of standards can support the overall improvement of accountability and performance.

The repeated message is that social and ethical accounting is not an easy answer to managing ethics. Nor is it an all-or-nothing process. But it aims, step by step, to provide a structure that assists the learning of the organisation and to drive improvement in performance.

Defining social and ethical

The terms "social" and "ethical" resonate differently with different audiences. For many, social issues concern the impact of a company on society, whereas ethical issues are typically understood as the broad range of concerns about companies' behaviour, relating to their values: their honesty, integrity and so on. For others, for example some of the ethical investment community, ethics concerns the core company product or service (pornography or fossil fuel perhaps) or its work practices (for example health and safety and diversity issues). To confuse matters, some organisations and consultants have used the terms "ethical accounting" and "social accounting" to refer to specific methodologies (often with much in common) that they have adopted or developed. This chapter brings together the terms social and ethical to refer jointly to the systems and individual behaviour within a company, as well as to the direct and indirect impact of these systems and behaviour on stakeholders.

What is social and ethical accounting and why do it?

Social and ethical accounting is a process that can help businesses (and other types of organisations) to address issues of accountability to stakeholders, and to improve performance: social, environmental and economic. The process typically links a company's values to the development of policies and performance targets and to the assessment and communication of performance. In this way, and through engagement with stakeholders, social and ethical issues are tied into a company's strategic management and operations.

But what are the issues, and who decides them? Social and ethical accounting is a model in which no specific group predetermines the issues that matter. There is no standardised balance sheet or unit of currency. Instead, the issues are defined by the company's values and aims, by the interests and expectations of its stakeholders, and by societal norms and regulations. With this focus on the concerns of society, the social and ethical accounting framework implicitly concerns itself with issues as wide as economic performance, working conditions, environmental and animal protection, human rights, fair trade and ethical trade, human resource management and community development, and hence with the sustainability of a company's activities.

Companies have begun to open themselves up to their stakeholders, partly because of the "push" factor of pressure group activity but also because they realise that a greater awareness of the impact of their activities and how they are perceived is necessary to improve strategic decision-making. More and more companies are now incorporating stakeholders in their decision-making processes. Much of this is, of course, standard business practice: talking to customers and suppliers to identify issues as they arise, to satisfy new needs and to resolve problems. But often a company realises that it is failing to involve important groups or there is mistrust or misunderstanding in its relations with stakeholders.

There is no one way
Each company's approach to social and ethical accounting has a different balance in terms of the issues it focuses on and the processes it uses to measure and communicate performance.

Some issues such as health and safety affect most businesses. Others, such as concern over genetically modified organisms, have a strong impact on specific sectors. This kind of pressure can be volatile, as shown by the movement of genetically modified organism (GMO) criticism along the value chain from Monsanto to Coca-Cola. Too often companies have been punished when they thought it could not happen to them.

In terms of process, some companies have developed codes of conduct and tried to measure how well these have been implemented. Others have tried to capture the financial value of their relationships and other intangible assets. Some have focused on communicating to employees or to local stakeholders, and others have made the impact of their overseas operations a priority.

Each company's approach will reflect its core functions and aims and the reasons it embarks on the social and ethical accounting process, and will be influenced by the legal requirements and societal norms of its areas of operations. The GMO issue illustrates how quickly societal pressures can change. And although changes in laws follow more slowly, companies should be aware of new developments: for example, the potentially profound changes in the investment market following the introduction of the Pensions and Investment Act in the UK requiring pension funds to state "the extent (if at all) to which social, environmental or ethical considerations are taken into account in the selection, retention and realisation of investments".

Other factors affecting the nature of social and ethical accounting include:

■ the ownership structure of the company;
■ the degree of sophistication of existing social and ethical measurement within the company;
■ the interest and demands of stakeholders, the history behind their relationship with the company and the importance with which each stakeholder group is viewed;
■ cost, time and resource pressures on the company;
■ uncertainty about the costs and benefits of the process;
■ the commitment of key individuals.

In short, the company has to understand not only what it wants to do, but also its capacities and the restrictions on its actions.

Principles of social and ethical accounting

Out of this diversity of approaches to social and ethical accounting there is an emerging consensus in business and society on the principles of best practice. These principles can be used in designing and managing a process, or in assessing its quality.

The dominant principle of social and ethical accounting is inclusivity. This principle requires that the aspirations and needs of all stakeholder groups are taken into account at all stages of the social and ethical accounting process.

Other principles can be put into three broad groups relating to the:

■ scope and nature of the company's social and ethical accounting process;
■ meaningfulness of the information created by the process;
■ continuous management of the process.

The principle of inclusivity influences each of these principles, as outlined below and based on AA1000, the accountability framework launched by the Institute of Social and Ethical Accountability in November 1999.

Scope and nature of the process
- **Completeness.** The inclusion in the accounting process of all appropriate areas of activity relating to an organisation's social and ethical performance.
- **Materiality.** The inclusion of significant information that is likely to affect stakeholder groups and their assessment of an organisation's social and ethical performance.
- **Regularity and timeliness.** The need for regular, systematic and timely action of the accounting process to support the decision-making of an organisation and its stakeholders.

Meaningfulness of information
- **Quality assurance.** The audit of an organisation's process by an independent and competent third party. The audit is concerned with building credibility (and providing assurance) in the process with all stakeholder groups, and hence developing meaningful stakeholder engagement.
- **Accessibility.** Appropriate and effective communication to an organisation's stakeholders of its accounting process and its performance.
- **Comparability.** The ability to compare information on an organisation's performance with previous periods, performance targets, or external benchmarks drawn from other organisations, statutory regulation or non-statutory norms.
- **Reliability.** The characteristic that allows an organisation and its stakeholders to depend on the information provided by the accounting to be free from significant error or bias.
- **Relevance.** The usefulness of information to an organisation and its stakeholders as a means of building knowledge and forming opinions, and as assistance to decision-making.
- **Understandability.** The comprehensibility of information to an organisation and its stakeholders, including issues of language, style and format.

Continuous management of the process
- **Embeddedness, or systems integration.** Making the accounting process part of an organisation's operations, systems and policy-making; that is, not just a one-off exercise to produce a report.
- **Continuous improvement.** Steps taken to improve performance in response to the results of the accounting process.

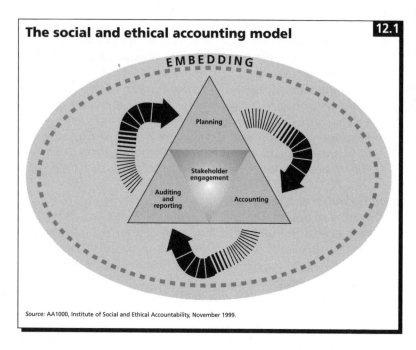

The social and ethical accounting model `12.1`

EMBEDDING

Planning

Stakeholder engagement

Auditing and reporting

Accounting

Source: AA1000, Institute of Social and Ethical Accountability, November 1999.

Putting principles into practice

But how do you put these principles into practice? The generic model of social and ethical accounting includes six elements in a continuing process that a business undergoes in order to manage and improve its accountability and performance. Drawn from the AA1000 framework, these are as follows (see also Figure 12.1).

- **Planning.** The company commits to the process of social and ethical accounting, auditing and reporting, and defines and reviews its values and social and ethical objectives and targets.
- **Accounting.** The scope of the process is defined, information is collated and analysed, and performance targets and improvement plans are developed.
- **Reporting.** A report on the company's systems and performance is prepared.
- **Auditing.** The process of preparing the report and the report itself are externally audited, and the report is made accessible to stakeholders in order to obtain feedback from them.
- **Embedding.** To support each of the stages, structures and systems

are developed to strengthen the process and to integrate it into the company's activities.
◪ **Stakeholder engagement.** The concerns of stakeholders are addressed at each stage of the process through regular involvement.

At every stage a company should incorporate useful experience from the previous cycle – it must be flexible enough to learn and innovate from the process.

Reporting in practice

The nature of social and ethical reporting is related to the size and nature of the organisation, as is the rest of the accounting process. For example, a small single-site company may distribute a single audited report on all aspects of its operations to its (mainly local) stakeholders. In contrast, a large, multinational company may seek to drive down responsibility for the measurement and improvement of performance to site level. It may then report at both site level (the aspects of performance relevant to local stakeholders) and group level (the overall activities and performance of the organisation), and may use a mixture of auditing methods to reflect the assurance required by stakeholders at each level. The following examples show how different companies take different approaches.

An energy company

The second approach is reflected in the reporting and accountability processes developed by Shell International. Shell's reports (*Profits and Principles: does there have to be a choice?* in 1998 and *People, planet and profit* in 1999, 2000 and 2001) have brought together economics, the environment and society. They have included an explanation of performance against each aspect, as well as key elements of governance and operations, including Shell's sustainable development management framework (SDMF) and a road map for measuring and managing progress towards sustainable development. The SDMF includes a framework that defines appropriate indicators and metrics to report at each stage of the company's operations: global, global/international, national and local. Shell believes that the appropriate medium of communication will vary for each level of reporting.

The sustainability report is not the end of the process. The SDMF includes a review stage to incorporate learning following the communication of performance. One input to this review will be the results of feedback to the Shell report and other communications. The Shell reports include comment cards, examples of which are included in the following year's report, and all of which, where permission is given, are placed on the Shell website.

A retail company

In its pioneering *Values Report* in 1997, The Body Shop International focused predominantly on its UK operations, and produced a single report on its policies and performance regarding social and ethical issues, the environment and animal rights. Its current programme of stakeholder communication, however, is based on stakeholder-specific reports delivered primarily through the Internet to each stakeholder group.

The Body Shop has also encouraged and supported accountability processes among its franchisees. In 1998, the Australia and New Zealand franchise produced a report that assessed performance and included detailed targets and actions for 2000 across social and ethical, environmental and animal protection issues. The lessons from this (and other) reporting processes have helped the company to begin to change relationships between the centre, the regions and stakeholders: "The corporate office will need to adopt a more executive role in overseeing the various accountability programmes in the regions and consolidating the key messages on a group-wide basis, [and] the nature of relationships between the Body Shop International and many of its stakeholders will evolve into different and potentially more intimate relationships with the regional head offices."

A financial services company

The UK's Co-operative Bank emphasises that its reports are not ends in themselves. They have a special purpose: they are part of the way the bank defines its values, as well as communicating these values and its performance in relation to them and related targets. The bank's report for 1998 gave a detailed explanation of its ethical policy development process, including stages of preparation, consultation, communication and implementation. The report for 1999 provides an audited examination of the implementation of these policies and the 2000 report, *Making our Mark*, provides detailed indicators of performance and targets. The bank's communications are therefore part of the process of building and strengthening values within the company and among its stakeholders.

This is social and ethical reporting aimed at the creation of long-term value. It is a way of talking to stakeholders; it helps the bank to make decisions; but more than this, the reporting (and the ethical decisions behind the reporting) is part of the way in which the bank defines its competitive advantage. Other companies may not use stakeholders as directly as the Co-operative Bank in selecting their values, but they can seek to gain the benefits of credibility and trust that come from reflecting the aspirations and needs of stakeholders. If the Co-operative Bank (or any other company) is to live up to its ethical statements and manage the risks to its reputation, it must ensure its employees will carry out these policies. It must embed its values from top to bottom.

Social and ethical accounting is not about perfection, but it begins with (and lives by) commitment.

Auditing in practice

However comprehensive and clear a report is, it needs to be trusted to be valuable. The media, investment analysts and pressure groups will always cast a sceptical eye over statements by companies about their social and ethical principles. Managers (and stakeholders) often mistrust the quality of the information they get. They want assurance that the company is performing as it should be, and that its activities are producing the desired outcomes. The need to build credibility and to establish a common understanding of performance has induced companies to audit their management processes and social and ethical reports.

The UK's 1999 Turnbull committee report emphasises the importance of internal audit in the management of risk. But an external audit process may be necessary to reassure stakeholders (including the company's managers) that the social and ethical accounting process is sound. The relationships between external audit, quality assurance and risk management are increasingly recognised by the major accountancy firms. KPMG, for example, believes that audits must focus "on understanding the business risks, processes and controls at both a strategic and an operational level", and that in order to meet the needs of the social audit process a more extensive published audit opinion will be required, perhaps covering:

- "the overall quality of a company's risk management processes;
- the overall scope and quality of the stakeholder dialogue processes;
- the overall quality of a company's internal assurance processes over all the information it provides;

◪ whether selected specific critical information is fairly stated."

Companies have embraced, or at least used, social and ethical auditing in a variety of forms. These have included auditing processes based on financial auditing practices (reporting a "true and fair" view) as well as innovative methods of providing quality assurance. As a new practice, and in the absence of auditing standards, the scope of the audits (in terms of issues, geographies, operations and stakeholders) has varied considerably. The audits have been completed by organisations with very different qualifications, using very different forms of audit opinion. This creates trepidation within some companies: what exactly are they paying for, and who will believe it? But in other cases it has helped to create innovative ways of deepening trust with stakeholders, and in so doing has reinforced the value of dialogue with society. The following example shows how one company adopted a range of approaches.

A *pharmaceuticals company*

Novo Group is involved in some of the most important and contentious business processes and product markets. These include the use of animal testing and GMOs in its insulin and enzyme production businesses.

Novo produces annual environmental and bioethics reports, and has been involved in stakeholder dialogue since the early 1990s, publishing its first social report in 1999. It identifies a driver of its reporting activities as being its understanding of its stakeholders, including consumer, environmental and biotechnology public-interest groups. It has said that engaging with its stakeholders over the years has not only given it a better awareness of their needs, but has also provided a major input to its strategy for sustainable development.

For its 1999 report, Novo embarked on a twin-track approach to auditing. The first part of the audit report focused on verifying data; the second part provided assurance to stakeholders concerning its activities, values, plans and outputs. A traditional accountancy firm carried out the data verification. It states in its report that the scope of the work did not constitute an audit in the sense of a financial audit, but it believes that the data included in the social report are consistent with documentation presented to it and that it has examined.

The second statement, which came from a consultant representing a non-profit organisation that has led in the development of social accounting, says that the aim is to "provide a broad perspective on the quality of published information and the underlying process of social accounting". It notes that Novo's report focuses more on stating where the business is, what it is and what it wants to be, rather than what its impacts are and are perceived to be. It also emphasises some of the company's key commitments to improve the social accounting process. But there is no formal opinion of, for example, the truth and fairness of the report.

Novo believes that the credibility of its results depends on using auditors that possess legitimacy with its different stakeholder groups. It also recognises that the audit process must be continuously reviewed and improved. For its latest report it has adapted the twin-track approach and brought in a panel of experts from business, academia and non-profit organisations to support the work of the independent auditors.

Novo is also represented on the governing council of the Institute of Social and Ethical Accountability, the professional body that addresses the issue of audit by developing the AA1000 assurance guidelines and forming a qualification for accountability professionals.

Stakeholder engagement in practice

Shell's experience with Brent Spar and in Nigeria, Nike's exposure for the use of child labour in Pakistan and criticism of Monsanto for its GMO products demonstrate the seriousness of understanding and responding to stakeholder concerns, and have led to more and more companies taking stakeholder engagement more seriously. The tricky bit is working out how best to do it.

Establishing a dialogue with stakeholders can help a company:

◪ anticipate and help manage conflicts;
◪ improve decision-making;
◪ build consensus among diverse views;
◪ create stakeholder identification with the outcomes of its activities.

Yet there is risk that engagement may add little value. Companies may worry about the:

◪ cost of engagement in time and other resources;
◪ risk of inviting criticism from stakeholders or the apathy of stakeholders;
◪ frequent failure of engagement to create a real change in performance;
◪ failure to engage with some of the stakeholders that really matter –

the weakest and those whom historically companies have known least about.

Any dialogue process is uncertain, with no guarantees. But lessons can be learned from the companies that have begun to engage more systematically with stakeholders. These suggest that if the engagement is to be productive, a company must be transparent in its intentions (making the purpose of the dialogue clear) and must demonstrate through its actions a commitment to improve in order to avoid disenchantment with the process. To help a company get a proper understanding of stakeholder aspirations and needs, the engagement process must:

- allow stakeholders to help identify other stakeholders who should be engaged;
- ensure that stakeholders trust whoever is collecting and processing information;
- be a genuine dialogue, not a one-way process;
- make sure that those involved are well-briefed about and have enough time to prepare for the engagement;
- involve stakeholders in defining the terms of the engagement;
- allow stakeholders to say exactly what they think without fear of penalty;
- make relevant information about different stakeholder groups available to each other and allow them to comment on it.

The nature and importance of standards

The variety of approaches adopted by companies in their social and ethical accounting and the experimentation involved has generated innovative techniques, yet weakened confidence in some processes. The adoption of accountability standards and guidelines that give advice to the organisation or define levels of performance helps introduce consistency into the process. Standards:

- provide a common language of best practice across companies and with stakeholders;
- make best practice more visible;
- inform the development of enabling legislation.

To be successful, the standards must facilitate innovation and flexibility in the management of social and ethical issues. They must allow leaders to lead but also bring along organisations new to the fields of accountability and sustainability. Furthermore, they need to work alongside other efforts to improve accountability and performance, including new management tools, new experiments in partnership, and initiatives to develop national and international legislation.

On the more negative side, companies have warned of a "sea of codes and standards" – a danger of confusion and of limited value-added. But the take-up of key standards demonstrates a recognition of their importance in supporting the management, measurement and communication of performance.

The variety of standards

Standards address both business process and business performance; there are standards focusing on single issues and standards encompassing a variety of issues; there are mandatory standards and voluntary standards. The processes they cover include stakeholder dialogue and social and ethical reporting; and the issues include organisational culture, fair trade and ethical trade, working conditions, human resource management and training, environmental and animal protection, community development and human rights.

A number of initiatives to develop common environmental systems and indicators gained wide currency in the 1980s and 1990s. These include the CERES principles, the PERI reporting guidelines, the ICC Business Charter for Sustainable Development, the UNEP/SustainAbility reporting ingredients, the World Business Council for Sustainable Development's eco-efficiency indicators, EMAS and the ISO14000 series.

The most innovative of recent standards (that widen the focus to social and economic issues) have been developed by multi-constituency partnerships between business, governments and international agencies, and civil society institutions. They have included the following.

THE GLOBAL REPORTING INITIATIVE (GRI): SUSTAINABILITY REPORTING GUIDELINES
These focus on a specific part of the social and ethical accounting process – reporting – although the GRI is exploring the role of verification guidelines to support its reporting process. The GRI defines a set of indicators of performance aiming to cover a full range of issues of concern to stakeholders, including social, environmental and economic issues, although these are currently at different stages of development. Following a pilot process, a revised version of the guidelines was launched in June 2000 (see www.globalreporting.org).

SOCIAL ACCOUNTABILITY INTERNATIONAL'S SOCIAL ACCOUNTABILITY 8000 (SA8000)
SA8000 has some aspects in common with the generic model identified in this chapter. Part of the standard concerns management systems and refers to the definition of policy, the monitoring of activities and results, the verification of conformance, the communication of procedures and the development of management systems. However, it focuses on a specific issue: working conditions in global supply chains (see www.cepaa.org).

THE ETHICAL TRADING INITIATIVE (ETI)
The ETI is a partnership of companies, unions and non-governmental organisations. Its base code focuses on a set of defined labour issues. Processes of accounting and embedding are defined by the requirement that suppliers of ETI members meet agreed standards, and that performance is measured, transparent and ultimately a precondition to further business. Members produce annual reports on progress against the code, and the ETI produces an annual summary report (see www.eti.org.uk).

THE INSTITUTE OF SOCIAL AND ETHICAL ACCOUNTABILITY: ACCOUNTABILITY 1000 (AA1000)
AA1000 is an accountability standard that can be used in two ways:

◪ To underpin the quality of specialised accountability standards, existing and emergent.
◪ As a process for managing and communicating social and ethical accountability and performance.

It gives companies (and other organisations) a standardised system that can support their processes of social and ethical accounting. This process is the basis of the generic model defined in this chapter. It seeks in particular to help companies understand the links between different standards and guidelines, as well as the links with other management tools, such as the balanced scorecard or the business excellence model. This supports the aim of social and ethical accounting to bring social and ethical issues into the heart of companies' strategic management and operations. The revision of AA1000 in 2001 introduces further practical guidance on issues of assurance, innovation, management systems and stakeholder engagement (see www.accountability.org.uk).

Following AA1000 (or another standard) will not remove the

complexity of managing social and ethical issues. Nor will it necessarily resolve a divergence of opinion between and within stakeholder groups. AA1000 can, however, help organisations by providing a process with which they can begin to address these issues. This is a process that brings ethics to the core of management by focusing on engagement with stakeholders as a way to understand what matters about performance.

Accountability standards should be considered in this context. They can provide a key element in a process of building credibility with stakeholders. But the commitment and leadership of the company cannot be left out: they are essential for the improvement of performance.

Conclusion

Social and ethical accounting, auditing and reporting are in their infancy, and best practice will continue to develop over the coming years. Companies have an opportunity to embrace this agenda either as leaders or by following the example of others in a step-by-step fashion.

In either case, social and ethical accounting provides a way in which companies can begin to assess their performance and bring the perspectives of stakeholders into this assessment. By tying social and ethical accountability processes into its strategy and operations, a company is able to measure its performance against what matters, both for itself and for its stakeholders. In so doing, it can begin to address a series of risks that may otherwise arise unseen and unchecked in each of these relationships.

13 Values-led regulation

David Jackman

A GOOD BUSINESS SHOULD BE BOTH COMPETITIVELY SUCCESSFUL AND A
FORCE FOR GOOD.

BP Amoco

OUR CORPORATE CULTURE IS THE SUM TOTAL OF WHAT WE BELIEVE AND
THINK, HOW WE WORK TOGETHER AS COLLEAGUES AND HOW WE
CONDUCT OURSELVES AS INDIVIDUALS. IT IS THE WAY WE TREAT OUR
CLIENTS, OUR SHAREHOLDERS, OUR FELLOW EMPLOYEES, OUR NEIGHBOURS
AND THE PUBLIC IN GENERAL. IT IS WHO WE ARE.

Merrill Lynch

FINANCIAL SERVICES HAS been one of the most pilloried industries in
recent years, thanks to a series of financial scandals involving
insider trading, rogue dealers, banking irregularities and incompetent
advice in financial markets around the world. The time-honoured
principle of self-regulation, and even governmental regulation in some
countries, has been seriously undermined. Many financial centres are
looking for more effective ways of policing their activities. While some
are opting for a more rigorous (and often complex and bureaucratic)
legal framework, other governments and financial centres are working
together to develop a middle way between self-regulation and
independent regulation.

In the UK, in particular, moves are well under way to create "value-
led" regulation, where firms are required to satisfy a simpler set of
regulations yet also encouraged to become more ethically accountable.
The organisation spearheading this new initiative is the Financial
Services Authority (FSA), created in 1997, which is responsible for banking
supervision and investment services regulation. This chapter uses the
FSA's experiences and approach to explore the thinking behind regulation
that is values-led and outlines the main steps necessary for such an
approach to be effective.

Regulation through rules: pros and cons

Every financial system must be underpinned by a rigorous legal framework. Regulation serves as a secure base line and reflects society's desire to balance or temper the financial services industry in some way. The public perception is that the industry's values are not sufficiently strong or secure to allow it to be self-governing or self-regulating.

An important component of a value-led approach is to keep developing a legal set of standards and requirements that reflect the realities of the financial services industry. However, legislation on its own is not enough to guarantee ethical business conduct. A rules-based approach and mentality invites a number of problems.

Rules do not guarantee results. Despite the best efforts to draft comprehensive and effective regulations, situations will arise that are not covered by the rules or guidelines. There will be grey areas, or times when an individual is unable to check the rights and wrongs of a proposed course of action.

When rules fail, values and ethical standpoints need to fill the gap. Ideally, individuals or firms would jump in a desirable direction on the basis of a set of internalised values and ethics. The stronger the ethical culture within a firm or within an industry as a whole, the more likely it is that a desirable outcome will be achieved. Peer pressure is a highly effective mechanism for maintaining and raising ethical standards.

Cracks also emerge when the rules cannot keep up with a fast-moving market, as is inevitable in an innovative and highly competitive environment. Again, an ethical platform is necessary to bridge gaps that appear.

Rules alone do not guarantee that firms buy into the values underpinning them. Although many rules are framed in terms of minimum standards, firms may implement them in a mechanical way or simply try to see what they can get away with, especially when in a grey area. This is where a focus on values is particularly helpful. It is unlikely that many firms welcome the idea of regulation, but they may well connect with the underlying values of fairness, respect, honesty and so on. So if it is doubtful that people will see the essential rightness of behaving in an ethical way, it may be more effective to encourage them to see the connection between ethical practice and good business sense. A firm that adopts and embeds essentially "professional" values will get fewer complaints from its customers and should therefore benefit commercially from an enhanced reputation.

Rules-based approaches encourage rules-based mentalities. This in turn encourages the delegation (in truth the abdication) of the responsibility of compliance to a small group of individuals within a legal or compliance function or department. Thus the whole enterprise of regulation becomes dependent on the competence and ethics of a few.

Developing value-led regulation

Value-led regulation is about changing the attitudes and approaches of individuals and cultures. This type of change cannot be forced; it can only come from within. Somehow, regulatory approaches must help firms to go beyond mere compliance to a more active engagement with the values underlying the legislation.

Governments, regulatory bodies and firms must be willing to work together in a process to uncover, challenge and develop a shared values system. For example, the core values that everyone wants to see operating effectively within the financial services industry are, typically:

- fairness;
- straightforwardness and absence of deception;
- responsibility, learning and accountability;
- consideration for others;
- trust and reliability.

This level of dialogue requires the discipline of thinking more deeply about implications and outcomes, rather than trying to impose rigid tenets, which only become a further set of worries to hang around managers' necks. The ability to turn common standards and values into shared ones constitutes the crucial difference between a genuine commitment to a set of ethical principles and mere lip service. If the regulator can give its employees and the industry it regulates a sense of the depth of its commitment, it will help achieve real strides towards a shared purpose.

Once a sense of shared purpose develops, a set of objectives will arise from and serve this purpose. For example, the FSA's overall purpose is to develop a financial system in which a set of values (including fairness, responsibility, accountability and so on) operate more effectively than under a system of self-regulation. Various objectives include:

- maintaining confidence in the British financial system;
- promoting public understanding of the financial system;
- securing the appropriate degree of protection for consumers;
- reducing the likelihood of financial crime.

A focus on values provides a unifying framework, drawing together various regulatory tools and approaches. A values-driven approach also helps regulators select the most appropriate tools for the job. The role of regulation becomes one of correcting, compensating for and developing an industry's values (professional competency must be viewed as part of being ethical). A values framework can then be used as a wrap-around to provide direction for regulatory bodies.

The role of the FSA

The regulatory environment in the UK is undergoing a sea change, partly as a result of a series of financial scandals, such as the huge losses made by a rogue trader at Barings and the misselling of pensions. Less spectacular, but equally influential, has been a strategic review involving political, regulatory and commercial organisations of the need for "a new regulator for the new millennium".

This debate resulted in the decision to create a single regulator for the UK's financial services industry. Formerly known as the Securities and Investments Board, this independent body was renamed the FSA in 1997 and given a wider set of powers and responsibilities. These are incorporated in the Financial Services and Markets Act, which was passed in June 2000 and implemented during 2001. The logic behind the act is to streamline and simplify legislation by having a single authority rather than some ten different regulators overseeing banking, building societies, insurance, personal investment, and securities and futures. The FSA's remit includes authorising firms and individuals, rulemaking, investigating, intervention powers and imposing financial penalties. It is also responsible for establishing and monitoring compliance with a code of market conduct.

The FSA aims to:

- make regulation a more transparent and open process;
- switch resources from reactive post-event action to front-end intervention;
- create incentives for firms to manage their own risks better and thereby reduce the burden of regulation.

The most important advantage of the creation of FSA is the opportunity to deal with the industry as a whole. The more generic issues are fundamentals of tone, attitude, culture, reputation and values. In essence, the FSA's vision is to develop the ethical culture and professional

13.1

The development of industry values and culture

	THE FSA'S ROLE	VALUES AND CULTURE
1 Minimum standards	*Policing* Detects problems/sample testing Respond to crises Enforcement ambulance Provides training on basic principles	Unthinking, mechanical compliance Does minimum can get away with Requires spoon feeding Culture of dependency Seeks prescription Abdicates some decisions to FSA
2 Aspirational culture	*Persuading/educating* Facilitates direction, pointers, establishes frameworks Provides structure of training Looks for warning signs Aims to bounce firms back on track Increases scope for focused visits, etc	Sound intentions and approach Reliant on guidance Aims to do more than minimum Buffer zone Implementation may be bureaucratic
3 Ethical culture	*Educating/consulting* Facilitates development of competence and culture Values scorecard/health checks Education Lighter touch – scope to reduce fees	Competence and ethical framework Effective systems and controls Risk focused, self-policing Buying in at senior level Ethos integrated into most business processes Ethos seen as assisting business
4 Sustainable regulation	*Mature relationship* Litmus testing Identifies good practice Leads by example Devotes resources to problem firms Sustainable cost of regulation	Internalises ethos of statutory objectives Spirit not just letter Goes beyond rules – not just compliance Well-developed individual responsibility and ownership by (all) staff Anticipates and deals with problems Prevention focus Continued reassessment and improvement of approach Awareness and discussion of ethical considerations at senior level Open relationship with FSA Strong learning culture

competence of the industry as a whole. Self-regulatory organisations (SROs) were good at maintaining established standards by weeding out problems and dealing with bad apples, but the FSA has the opportunity to focus on raising standards within and across the industry. It can focus its regulatory tools on consciously improving ethics, values and culture.

The FSA uses a development model that correlates the values and culture of a firm or sector with the most appropriate type of relationship that the authority should have with them. The framework indicates how to develop a firm's or a sector's values and culture by moving through:

- unthinking compliance to minimum standards;
- an aspirational culture – aiming to do more than the minimum;
- an ethical culture – effective systems and controls exist;
- internalised statutory objectives, leading to a mature relationship with the FSA and enabling "sustainable regulation".

See Table 13.1.

As a firm exhibits a more ethical culture its relationship with the FSA evolves. The model allows both the "bank" role of supervision and the "SRO" approach of enforcement to work together, possibly with one phasing in as the other recedes. This allows regulators to embrace existing approaches in a wider model rather than feeling compelled to converge towards a middle way. Interventions through supervision, enforcement and so on can be geared to developing values and culture and maturing the relationship between the FSA and the industry (and other stakeholders).

When firms reach the stage of ethical maturity the FSA can step back. A value-led approach allows a regulator to recognise that a firm with a healthy ethos needs less attention and resources. As ethics comes to the fore, regulations can recede to become part of the normal business processes. Regulation can then become sustainable, enabling the FSA to concentrate its resources on problem firms. This is a familiar concept, but a values perspective allows for the rationale to be connected back to the purpose.

The model aims to move firms away from mechanical compliance and towards self-regulation and accountability. This means that regulators should shape their interventions in such a way as to try and improve the way firms behave. It makes no sense to identify weaknesses, and even possibly take disciplinary action, without the firm understanding what it should have done in the first place or knowing how or why it should improve.

This requires a holistic approach to risk assessment and brings to the fore indicators of values and culture. The model developed by Arthur Andersen and London Business School in their report *Ethical Concerns and Reputation Risk Management* (described in Chapter 2) suggests the internal processes that need to be in place to help firms reach the point where they can have open relationships with external regulators (see Figure 2.2, page 35).

Training and competence: a litmus test

Education is an important tool for the FSA in its task of helping firms manage their own ethical risks better and thereby reduce the burden of regulation. Professional competence should involve ethical competence. After extensive industry-wide consultation, the FSA introduced a new training and competence regime for advisers during 2000 to replace an overly complicated and bureaucratic set of rules and guidance.

If firms are to feel committed to training and developing their staff, and individuals are to feel committed to playing their part in learning, the FSA needs to remove the hindrances and obstructions that put people off or confuse the message. It has therefore reduced its requirements to a minimum. Firms are required to put training strategies and audits in place to ensure that:

- they recruit and appropriately employ appropriately skilled staff;
- they provide continuing training;
- their employees attain competence and pass the relevant professional examinations;
- their employees maintain their competence;
- they monitor and supervise employees' competence.

The introduction of these few simply stated requirements means that firms can no longer cite unnecessary bureaucracy and obfuscation as an excuse for inaction. Five rules that matter (and can be understood and remembered) are more effective rather than 50 that confuse.

The FSA uses every opportunity to encourage firms to think about their training strategy as well as providing basic practical tools to assist firms in making the journey. For example, it has produced a toolkit template to assist trade associations to develop similar toolkits for their members. These typically consist of detailed sector-specific material encompassing:

- market norms and accepted market practice;

- practical examples and models of procedures, methodologies and documentation;
- best-practice case studies of training and competence policies and arrangements.

Although many of the rules and much of the guidance about training and competence will be familiar to independent financial advisers, the five rules or commitments are deliberately high level. It is up to firms to decide on the most appropriate training and supervisory processes. This approach removes the comfort blanket of detailed prescription and makes it impossible for firms to aim low by doing solely what the regulator asks. Firms have to think through for themselves what the appropriate level of training should be, how it should be assessed and how competence should be maintained. By encouraging managers and professionals to think for themselves, real cultural change may follow.

Mechanical compliance, or a box-ticking mentality, almost by definition requires minimum thought. It is a fair assumption that if a firm has had difficulty thinking through its training strategy, it will also have difficulty thinking through other aspects of compliance. Training and competence become a good litmus test of a firm's overall compliance culture.

Working in partnership with related bodies is another important way of raising standards of competence and professionalism within the financial services industry. The FSA has a close dialogue with the national training organisations in the sector, the qualification and curriculum authorities, trade associations, professional bodies and institutes to help develop appropriate support materials and to ensure that qualifications are relevant.

This approach to training and competence demands much of the industry, firms and individuals and also of the regulator. But it means that the FSA is deeply engaged in the process of change from the bottom up, and it provides the industry with a perfect opportunity to express and demonstrate its professionalism.

Getting your house in order

Any regulator that wants the industry it regulates to develop a certain set of values and behave according to certain standards must live out those values and behave according to those standards. There is no getting round this; human nature detects and dislikes double standards. But a value-led approach will help a regulator to develop its operations as well as helping the firms it regulates to develop their operations.

Value-led regulation requires the regulator to practise what it preaches by:

- identifying its own values;
- developing and aligning these values – first internally, then externally;
- reinforcing these values and purposes and providing leadership within the industry.

The FSA is clear about its ultimate purpose of serving the public good. People join it because they want to make a difference and care, at least to some extent, about these values. It will do itself harm if it pretends to be something it is not. For example, it is not a commercial organisation, although it may find it helpful to learn some commercial disciplines. Its bottom line is essentially an ethical bottom line. It should be a force for good, and its added value is successfully increasing this overall sum of good. An awareness of these underlying values helps to shape its culture and define its identity.

The most effective way of transmitting values is seeing them demonstrated by another person or organisation. The way in which FSA staff conduct themselves on visits, carry out the first few enforcement actions, communicate with stakeholders and so on sets the tone for building relationships of trust and effective dialogue.

The FSA has, in effect, a leadership role in developing and supporting the values inherent in the act under which it was established. In the jargon, it needs to walk the talk and to do so consistently. This means it must have a coherent view of these values internally, as well as seeing how they can be applied in practice. But although values must be internalised, any alignment of them cannot be forced but has to be developed sensitively and carefully. A regulator not asking why is *as* great a risk as firms not asking why.

Conclusions

Chris Moon and Clive Bonny

THE CORRELATION BETWEEN BUSINESS ETHICS AND THE BOTTOM LINE IS A FREQUENT THEME IN A NUMBER OF STUDIES. FOR EXAMPLE, A STUDY BY ROMAN, HAYIBOR AND AGLE (BUSINESS AND SOCIETY, 1999) EXAMINES SUCH A RELATIONSHIP BY ANALYSING AND RECLASSIFYING EXISTING LITERATURE AND RESEARCH DONE OVER THE PAST 25 YEARS. OF THE 51 RECLASSIFIED STUDIES, 33 WERE FOUND TO SHOW A POSITIVE RELATIONSHIP BETWEEN ETHICS AND CORPORATE FINANCIAL PERFORMANCE.

Center for Business Ethics News, Winter 2001

THERE IS EVIDENCE that business is facing up to ethical issues. Clearly unethical conduct can damage a firm's reputation and hit its bottom line and the share price. In some cases it can even force a company out of business. Just one legal transgression can cost a company millions of dollars and firms that do not have ethics programmes run the risk of more stringent penalties than those that do. Furthermore, bad publicity can have a profound impact on brand value and a business's ability to attract and retain the best people, thus eroding its competitive edge.

On the other hand, companies who apply ethical auditing and measure their triple bottom line – economic, environmental and social sustainability – are shown by independent studies to have outperformed since 1990 other s&p 500 index companies. Not only does an ethical approach increase shareholder value but other stakeholders gain too. Organisations that measure and respond to staff feedback on culture and motivation regularly outperform their competitors. This has been revealed by employee surveys of the best companies to work for. Trust and openness also strengthens supplier and customer partnerships, and engenders community respect and integration.

Different countries have taken different approaches to business ethics. The United States has taken a more compliance-based approach and has led the way in the international criminalisation of bribery of public officials, legislation that the OECD has recently endorsed. Europe's approach to business ethics has been less regulatory-based than that of the United States but recent European human rights legislation has widened the scope of organisations' responsibilities towards their stakeholders. In North America the role of the ethics officer has been formalised, while in Europe ethics champions have developed their roles alongside their other management responsibilities.

Two other international differences are becoming less marked. The western preference for business unit autonomy and the eastern practice of economic networking are coming together. Japanese and Korean industrial conglomerates have, for many years, successfully interlocked family, private and public business networks. This has demonstrated to those in the West how such connectivity can bring greater operational efficiency and more consumer choice. The benefits of teamwork, however, can only be unlocked by values and behaviours that support group goals and minimise internal competitiveness. This book argues that the integration of the more formal compliance-based approach with a values-based approach, together with an acceptance of both the importance of the individual and respect for the team, creates the mix necessary for sustainable success.

The new economy has brought greater transparency and greater flexibility but also greater complexity – and therefore new and greater risks. Companies need to have robust systems in place to manage reputation risks. Employees who have more power in delayered organisations and more pressures to perform in a globally competitive environment have less management supervision. Only 42% of employees are reported to feel allegiance to their employer, and access to communications technology makes it easy for an individual anywhere in the world to damage a brand's international reputation in a matter of days, if not hours. Surveys show that 50% of employees trawl the web at work for personal reasons; 85% use the company computer for personal mail. This can lead to loss of intellectual property, inadvertent contracting, system viruses and libellous messages being sent that identify the organisation from whose computer they have come. Most firms do little to monitor their Internet traffic, yet over 90% of employees would accept company monitoring if introduced after consultation.

To ensure that there is trust and accountability managers must create a climate that will allow those they manage to make responsible decisions aligned within a framework of shared standards and consistent values. Clear standards of operation and behaviour are necessary to draw the lines between acceptable and unacceptable conduct. Constitutions and codes create the building blocks of acceptable behaviour. They should be drawn up in consultation with all those in the supply chain and presented in a way that people understand and accept. Such frameworks need to reinforce local and international regulations, be tailored for each business, and be checked in their application for gaps between what is said and what is done. Codes of conduct, however, will not, by themselves, ensure ethical practice. There must be commitment behind them and they must be shown to work. Auditing their effectiveness requires competent and independent help.

Corporate social responsibility is being encouraged by a new breed of active shareholders who have been helped by greater transparency and regulation, such as disclosure laws on pension funds and increased legal responsibilities and liabililities for managers and directors. The annual general meeting has become much more prone to unexpected shareholder resolutions and activists determined to make their point in their pursuit of getting companies to balance private profit with public good.

A coherent self-regulatory approach to business ethics requires those with a stake in a firm and its activities to believe in the same ethical principles and values – and for those principles and values to be explicit and linked to the firm's brands. The process of defining what those principles and values are needs to be driven and championed by top management, and developed and assessed in a structured way. Opinions about a firm should be sought from customers, suppliers and the wider community. Line managers and other employees should be asked their views about the values demonstrated inside the business. Survey results should be published and stakeholders actively engaged in addressing the gaps they reveal between the reality of what people think about an organisation and what the organisation wants people to think about it. These gaps represent risk to brand integrity and are often caused by ineffective corporate communications or poor individual skills in decision-making. Training programmes can help resolve the latter.

Training in business ethics provides the opportunity for discussion and group commitment to achieve a consistent way of working. Yet only three in five organisations that provide ethical training for employees provide it for all employees. Training can also resolve difficult personal decisions and help employees understand corporate values.

Business ethics involves many tricky issues and there is no single best route to ensuring that an organisation deals effectively with them. The supply chain is as strong as its weakest link and shared values act as the glue to hold people together across different nations and cultures. One strong message of this book is that an "inside-out" approach that considers issues from employees outward is likely to be most successful.

Business ethics is about ensuring acceptable standards of behaviour throughout all the operations of a business wherever they are. There may be short-term costs involved when a business raises its ethical game but, in the longer term, businesses that are trusted and respected by their employees, suppliers, customers and the wider community are more likely than businesses that are not to provide their shareholders with a better return and to be sustainable.

REFERENCES

References

Chapter 1

1 Quoted directly from "Telling All About Internet Monitoring Policy Can Keep Your Office Litigation-Free", *PR NEWS*, Vol. 56 Issue 3, January 26th 2000.

2 Adapted from Boughton, I., "No such thing as a private e-mail", *Guardian*, September 4th 2000.

3 Adapted from Sipior, J.C. and Ward, B.T., "The dark side of employee email", *UMI Association for Computing Machinery Communication*, July 1st 1999 (© Association for Computing Machinery, July 1999).

4 Source: NFO Worldwide survey for Elron Software, adapted from *PR NEWS*, op. cit.

5 Adapted from Rolfe, J., "Office email abusers run riot", *Daily Telegraph (Sydney)*, March 24th 2000 (© Nationwide News Proprietary Ltd, 2000).

6 Source: NFO Worldwide survey for Elron Software, adapted from *PR NEWS*, op. cit.

7 Adapted from *PR NEWS*, op. cit.

8 Adapted from Boughton, op. cit.

9 Quoted directly from *PR NEWS*, op. cit.

10 Source: Matthew Boyle, "So where do MBAs want to work", *Fortune*, April 16th 2001.

11 Source: Chambers, E.G., Foulon, M., Hadfield-Jones, H., Hankin, S.M. and Michaels III, E.G., "The war for talent", *The McKinsey Quarterly*, No. 3, 1998, pp. 44–57.

12 Adapted from *The Citizen* (Gloucester), "Changing jobs to get to the top?", May 17th 2000 (© The Citizen, 2000).

13 Quoted in O'Malley, M.N., "Creating Commitment: How to Attract and Retain Talented Employees by Building Relationships That Last", John Wiley & Sons, April 14th 2000, Chapter 1.

14 www.cluetrain.com.

15 Adapted from "The 100 Best Companies to Work For", *Fortune*, January 10th 2000 (© Time Inc.).

16 Quoted directly from *Fortune*, op. cit.

17 Department of Trade and Industry, *Our competitive future: building*

the knowledge driven economy, December 1998, p. 7.

18 Richard Boulton, Barry Libert, Steve Samek, *Cracking the Value Code: How Successful Business are Creating Wealth in the New Economy*, New York, HarperCollins, 2000.

19 Quoted in "A New Vision for Business", available at www.business-impact.org.

Chapter 2

1 "Managing Ethics and Legal Compliance: What Works and What Hurts?" *California Management Review*, Volume 41, Number 2, Winter 1999.

2 *Ethical Concerns and Reputation Risk Management, a study of leading UK companies*, Andersen, 1999.

3 These findings are supported in a recent review of 52 studies by Ronald M. Roman, Sefa Hayibor, and Bradley R. Agle, "The Relationship Between Social and Financial Performance: Repainting a Portrait", *Business & Society*, Vol. 38, Number 1, pp. 109–125. Sage Periodicals Press, March 1999.

4 *IntraSight™Assessment* was developed by Andersen in this regard in order to provide a more objective understanding of the ethical culture of an organisation.

Chapter 3

1 For further discussion see Driscoll, D-M., Hoffman, W.M. and Murphy, J.E., "Business Ethics and Compliance: What Management Is Doing and Why", *Business and Society Review*, No. 99, July 1998, pp. 35–51.

2 Ibid.

3 *United States Sentencing Guidelines*, Washington, DC, November 1st 1991, Chapter 8 "Sentencing of Organizations".

4 In Re Caremark International Inc. Derivative Litigation, 1996 WL 549894, (Del. Chancery C.A. 13670, September 15th 1996).

5 Founded in 1976, the Center for Business Ethics at Bentley College, Waltham, Massachusetts, is one of the oldest and most internationally recognised institutes for the study and exchange of ideas in business ethics.

6 Daly, F.J., "Rules and Values are Ethical Allies", *CBE News*, Vol. 2, Issue 2, Summer 1998.

7 See Driscoll, D-M. and Hoffman, W.M., *Ethics Matters: How to Implement Values-Driven Management*, Center for Business Ethics,

Waltham, MA, 2000. The first time Driscoll and Hoffman developed this ten-point programme was in *Long-Range Planning*, Vol. 32, No. 2, 1999, pp. 179–189.

8 Kaplan, J., Murphy, J. and Swenson, W., *Compliance Programs and the Corporate Sentencing Guidelines*, Clark Boardman Callaghan, Deerfield, IL, 1993.

9 See Driscoll, D-M. and Hoffman, W.M., "Doing the Right Thing: Business Ethics and Boards of Directors", *Director's Monthly*, No. 18, November 1994, pp. 1–7; Driscoll, D-M. and Hoffman, W.M., "Hark Corporate Director: "Tis the Call of Ethical Leadership", *Ethics Today*, No. 3, Winter 1998, p. 5; and Driscoll, D-M. and Hoffman, W.M., "Ethics and Leadership from the Top," *ASCI Journal of Management*, Spring 1999, pp. 23–32.

10 These factors need not be complex. "What would I advise my child to do?" "How would this look in the newspaper?" "If my decision were to set a precedent, what would be the result?" are examples of mini-tests of an ethical course of action.

11 See Driscoll, D-M., "The hazards of blowing the whistle", *Boston Business Journal*, July 5th–11th 1996, p. 8.

12 Kaplan, J., "Sundstrand's 'Responsible Executive' Program", *Corporate Conduct Quarterly*, No. 4, 1996, p. 33.

13 Examples of these behaviours include "Confronts and deals with integrity issues", "Leads by example", "Shows respect for suppliers as team members" and "Stands up for what he/she believes in". Driscoll, D-M., Hoffman, W.M. and Petry, E.S., *The Ethical Edge: Tales of Organizations That Have Faced Moral Crises*, MasterMedia Ltd, New York, 1995, pp. 153–157.

14 Purdy, K., "Who's doing what? – A look at industries and companies", *Ethical Management*, Vol. 7, No. 11, 1998, pp. 5–6.

15 Beatty, J., *The World According to Peter Drucker*, The Free Press, New York, 1998, p. 10.

16 Davis, W.F., "Managing Ethics in Today's Changing Utility Industry", The Sears Lectureship in Business Ethics, Center for Business Ethics, Bentley College, November 2nd 1999, p. 15.

Chapter 4

1 For a full explication of this four-step process, see Kidder, R.M., *How Good People Make Tough Choices: Resolving the Dilemmas of Ethical Living*, Simon & Schuster, New York, 1996.

2 Handy, C., "Trust and the Virtual Organization", in Reichheld, F.F.,

The Quest for Loyalty: Creating Value through Partnership, Harvard Business Review Books, Cambridge, MA, 1996, p. 40.

3 Dalla Costa, J., *The Ethical Imperative: Why Moral Leadership is Good Business*, HarperCollins, New York, 1998, p. 232.

4 Levering, R. and Moskowitz, M., *The 100 Best Companies to Work for in America*, Currency/Doubleday, New York, 1993.

5 Quoted in Cooper, R. and Sawaf, A., *Executive EQ: Emotional Intelligence in Leadership & Organizations*, Grosset/Putnam, New York, 1996, p. 87.

6 Handy, op. cit., p. 32.

7 Ibid., p. 36.

8 Fukuyama, F., *Trust: The Social Virtues and the Creation of Prosperity*, New York, The Free Press, 1995, pp. 27–28.

9 Kidder, R.M., *Shared Values for a Troubled World: Conversations with Men and Women of Conscience*, Jossey-Bass, San Francisco, 1994, pp. 309–320.

10 See Kidder, op.cit., pp. 66–73.

11 *Ethical concerns and reputation risk management*, Andersen in association with London Business School, London, 1999, p. 17.

12 See Kidder, op. cit., pp. 109–150.

13 See Kidder, op. cit., pp. 154–163.

14 *Global Values, Moral Boundaries: A Pilot Survey*, Institute for Global Ethics, Camden, Maine, 1997.

Chapter 5

1 Collins J. and Porras, J., *Built to Last – Successful Habits of Visionary Companies*, Century Hutchinson, 1998.

2 *RSA Inquiry into Tomorrow's Company*, Gower, 1995.

3 Co-operative Bank, *Partnership Report 2000*, p. 22.

4 Ibid., p. 2.

5 Merck and Company, *Internal Management Guide*, 1989.

6 Hampden Turner, C. and Trompenaars, F., *The Seven Cultures of Capitalism*, Currency Doubleday, 1993.

7 Hampden Turner, C. and Trompenaars, F., *Building Cross Cultural Competence: How to Create Wealth from Conflicting Values*, John Wiley, 2000, p. 1.

8 LaBarre, P., "The Company without Limits", *Fast Company Magazine*, September 1999, p. 160.

9 Ibid.

10 Ibid.

11 Interview with Amanda Hall, *Sunday Telegraph*, August 27th 2000.

12 Watson, T.J. Junior, *Father Son and Co: My Life at IBM and Beyond*, Bantam 1990, p. 404.

13 This case study was kindly provided by Steve Mullins of Gerard International. The authors are indebted to Gerard International for their help in reviewing drafts of this chapter and contributing to the development of their thinking.

14 Jackson, T., *Inside Intel*, HarperCollins, 1997.

15 Ibid., pp. 70–71.

16 Ibid., p. 72.

17 Ibid., Chapter 39.

18 Ibid., Chapter 40.

Chapter 6

1 "Corporate responsibility: doing well by doing good", *Independent Director* newsletter, IoD/Ernst & Young, No. 5, spring 2001.

2 Lone, Z., "The key questions non-executives should ask about CSR", *Independent Director* newsletter, IoD/Ernst & Young, Spring 2001.

3 Wilson, A. and Gribben, C., "Business Responses to Human Rights", April 2000.

4 *Financial Times*, 28 February 2001.

5 "Ethics on the agenda", *Independent Director* newsletter, winter 2000/1.

6 "Modern company law for a competitive economy: the strategic framework", February 1999, p. 37.

7 *The Economist*, 19 June 1993.

8 Rushton, K., "Cracking the code", IoD Directors guide: *Sustainable Development*, May 2001.

9 "The link between financial performance and corporate citizenship", 1999.

10 *The Times*, 17 May 2001.

11 "Review of UK company codes of conduct", DFID, 1998.

Chapter 8

Jane Nelson and Frances House are grateful for the help given by Joanne Barr and John Phillips in writing this chapter, the contents of which were drawn mainly from two publications:

Frances House and Peter Frankenthal, *Human rights – is it any of your business*, published by The Prince of Wales Business Leaders Forum

(PWBLF) in association with Amnesty International UK, April 2000. Jane Nelson, *The business of peace – the private sector as a partner in conflict prevention and resolution*, published by the PWBLF in association with International Alert and the Council on Economic Priorities, September 2000.

Website: www.pwblf.org

Chapter 9

1 Transparency International is the Berlin-based coalition against corruption, which now has more than 75 national chapters in developed, developing and transitional countries. Its website is at www.transparency.org.

Chapter 11

1 Donaldson, T., *The Ethics of International Business*, Oxford University Press, 1989.
2 Tabaksblat, M., *Dialogue Within Society*, Unilever, 1997.
3 Webley, S., *Codes of Ethics and International Business*, Institute of Business Ethics, London, 1997.
4 www.unglobalcompact.org
5 www.cauxroundtable.org
6 www.globalsullivanprinciples.org
7 Included in: Treasure, J., *Business Responsibilities*, Foundation for Business Responsibilities, NTC Publications Ltd.